Communism Through My Eyes: My Father

To my Angel of light!
Carolyn, meet my father,
Robert. Trujillo and
in doing so may we
continue to spread
light, peace, and
Love to our
world!

♡
Mary Lou Salazar

Communism Through My Eyes: My Father

Robert Trujillo
(1903-1986)

ISBN-10: 0-7178-0751-7   ISBN–13: 978-0-7178-0751-2
Typeset by Amnet Systems, Chennai, India

Table of Contents

Preface

Robert Trujillo was a revolutionary, a visionary, and a common man. He was a native of Colorado, born into a poor working-class family in the San Luis Valley, a Mexican American and a devout Catholic for the first 30 years of his life. The Great Depression hit in 1929, throwing Robert and millions of other laborers in America out of work. It had devastating effects on people throughout the nation. It was the worst depression in the history of U.S. capitalism.

Robert found himself stuck in a mass of debris and total despair. With a wife and three children, he allied himself with the unemployed and began organizing and leading them to demand jobs in Walsenburg, Colorado. Exposed to the Communist Party by literature he was receiving from the National Unemployed Council, he joined the Colorado Communist Party and later became its Chairman. He remained a communist for the rest of his life.

Communism Through My Eyes: My Father, Robert Trujillo was written by me to share, inform, and educate people about the plight of workers and their historical contributions and impact in Colorado and around the nation. In and out of jail, facing a lifetime of opposition and a series of crises fighting prejudice and racism throughout his life, he never stopped speaking for those without a voice. I lived with, loved, and respected the man for his heart, his devotion, and his courage, even though many considered him the enemy. For me he was the light of hope.

Mary Lou Salazar

Acknowledgements

I started this book not realizing the number of people who would contribute to it. Sincere appreciation is offered to the following people for sharing their views and ideas and for giving me inspiration: Craig Hart for his dedication to peace and justice; Ricardo Lafore, Lalo Delgado, Magdalena Gallegos, Barbara Revelle, and all the relatives and friends and reporters who respected my father, Robert Trujillo. My deepest thanks to each of them for allowing me into their lives and for enriching mine. A special thanks goes to Aunt Della and Aunt Frances, Dad's younger sisters, for their stories about my father. Thanks are in order to my brothers and sisters for their contributions: Frank, Ruth, Fred, Pete, Orlanda, Rena, and Richard; and to my sisters-in-laws: Julie for her interview with my mother, Edna, and Angie for her constant encouragement. Thank you also, Jack S. Blawis, for copyright permission on Autobiography of Pat Bell-Blau. A special acknowledgment goes to my beloved brother Gil, who passed away in 1981, and to my beautiful sister Marina (Rena), who passed away in 1999 and who wrote loving thoughts in her unpublished memoirs about our father. In some cases I have eliminated names to protect the individuals.

A special thanks goes to Dr. Vincent C. de Baca for his expertise and critical first reading, which gave me a jumpstart, to my dear friend, Chris Gabrielson, for editing and for her years of loving support and friendship; to my soul sister Dr. Jioanna Carjuzaa for her reviews and recommendations, to

Richard Gould whose proofreading helped to keep me moving towards completion. A special thanks goes to Dr. Michael S. Cummings for his years of support and friendship and for his expertise in the final editing.

I am grateful to and appreciate my children: my firstborn daughter, for her story and whose love, empathy, strength, and accomplishments have awakened the spirit in me; my son, for his love and sharing, and his incredible life of risk-taking which has inspired me to take my own risks; my daughter-in-law, whose love, compassion, and belief in me are evident in her own successes; my youngest daughter, for her story and whose love, work with students, and creativity have stimulated my own; my son-in-law, whose love and friendship I truly treasure; to my beautiful grandchildren: for my first granddaughter who was my biggest cheerleader, and for her delightful stories, my grandson and five granddaughters and three great grandsons and five great granddaughters. To all of them, I dedicate this story of their grandfather, great grandfather, and great-great grandfather Robert, so that each of them may reach for their own goals, while cultivating his values of love, peace, and justice.

A special thanks goes to my beloved parents, Robert and Edna Trujillo, whose spirits are in me, whose love for peace and justice inspired me to write this book, and to my beautiful first family: my brothers and sisters, whose faith in me kept the candle burning.

I am especially grateful to my beloved late husband, Virgil, for his contribution, incredible energy, encouragement, patience, and faith in me, loving support, and his wonderful sense of humor. My husband of forty-two years passed to spirit in 2001. His spirit of immense love keeps my fire burning, as it runs through the veins of each of our children, grandchildren, and great grandchildren.

Foreword

The Cold War has ended and the Soviet Union has been dissolved, I go back in time to try to understand, first, why a Mexican American became a communist in America and, second, why and how he remained one throughout his adult life.

This book is about Robert Trujillo, a political leader who helped shape Colorado. Robert was a humanitarian, a grassroots activist, and a leader of the Colorado Communist Party. He was an astute and critical thinker who focused on the trends and needs of the times. He was my father. The unconventional experience of growing up with him has shaped and influenced my entire life.

As the youngest daughter (I have one younger brother of his nine children), I write the story of his life as seen through my unique lens. The most important lesson I learned from my father is this: that love moves one to action. In this vein I offer his story to you, my readers.

I am not writing to make my father a hero, because he does not need such idealization. He was a leader, but he was human, with flaws as well as virtues. He was a man of enormous passion and compassion, which stemmed from his deep love of humanity. He was a champion of the working class and the poor, whose voices are seldom heard.

Prologue

Robert Trujillo was a product of the Great Depression. In 1929, when he lost his job in the coal mine, he experienced suffering and desperation first hand, along with millions of other Americans who were common laborers. His passion for justice and truth gave him the courage to be different. It led him to choose the path of communism. Robert spent his entire adult life trying to improve conditions for people; many benefited from his efforts.

I lived with and loved the man and the communist. Because the path he chose was considered that of "the enemy," he was even more fascinating to me. He was also my friend. Seldom have I met another with his depth, empathy, and love. His eyes sparkled with that love. Years after his death, writers still remember and write about him, and his words still ring loudly.

This book is a story that includes the voices of different people and focuses on their personal, intellectual, and emotional experience with Robert. The images of others therefore described in this writing are definitely not neutral, but they are authentic.

My father left me both a treasure chest and the key. I open it to share with you.

Introduction

My father, Robert, is one of the faces of history on the mural at the new convention center in downtown Denver. The mural, by Barbara Jo Revelle, "A People's History of Colorado," is 600 feet long and is made of 300,000 one-inch industrial tiles in shades of black, white, and gray. From among hundreds of nominations, 84 women and 84 men were chosen for the mural.

Picture of mural, Robert is the 4th person (middle) bottom.

1

Barbara Jo Revelle spoke at the celebration honoring Robert Trujillo:

> From everything I've read, what he believed in was humanity and human rights, and that's what we wanted to honor him for by including him in the mural. Still, Trujillo's inclusion in the mural generated a great deal of controversy. It took five months of fighting with the city fathers. "Do we have to have a Black Panther (Lauren Watson)?" they would say, and "This guy [Robert Trujillo] was a Communist!"

The photo that I selected to be displayed on the mural was symbolic, because it was representative of the Depression era, when Robert was immersed in the struggle. My heart filled with pride when I saw the mural for the first time. I thought, "He is finally getting recognition instead of opposition for his life's work." To me the recognition was not just his own; it represents the poor and all those who are not given a voice.

A flash of Robert as a child came to me, picturing him as a little Catholic boy trying to understand his teachings from his home and the church. He had an extraordinary mind, questioning why the values and standards he was taught didn't apply to the wealthy. He saw many contradictions in society, including the injustices all around him. He saw how poor his family was, with holes in their shoes, and he compared his life to that of the large farm owners who lived in big beautiful homes and seemed to have everything. I am always amazed when I realize that although Robert was born into the faceless anonymity of poverty, he became in the eyes of many, a respected humanitarian leader of the voiceless poor during the Depression. Then, later, serving the poor and underserved, he became the compassionate and courageous leader of the Colorado Communist Party.

On October 19, 1903, Robert Trujillo was born in Chama, in the San Luis Valley in southern Colorado. "I was born on that day," he said, "but I was not fully alive until I was thirty years old, at which time I became a radical and, thereafter, a revolutionary." He joined the Communist Party of the state of

Colorado in 1936. He remained a Communist for the rest of his life.

His layoff from the coal mine in Walsenburg, Colorado in 1929 propelled him into a life of activism. With a wife and small children and faced with extreme poverty, he became involved in the struggle for the right to work or to receive public assistance if jobs were not available. During the Great Depression, he was state president of the Workers Alliance of America. He was jailed in Trinidad, Colorado, for addressing an unemployed-workers rally in front of the Las Animas County courthouse. A county judge set him free. He was again jailed, in 1940, in Walsenburg for leading a parade of the unemployed "without a permit."

A county judge sentenced him to serve thirty days in jail. Dad appealed his case to the Colorado Supreme Court. The Supreme Court declared the Walsenburg City Charter, under which he was arrested, unconstitutional, and he won his case. After these experiences, Robert became even more aware of his deepening political passion, and he remained in the workers' struggle.* [See Supreme Court Case, Trujillo vs. city of Walsenburg, page 163 in Appendix.]

First and foremost, he believed in the philosophy of Christ that he had inherited from his Catholic upbringing: To love his neighbor as his brother and to do unto others, as he would have them do unto him. He felt that sharing the resources of the world was the best path for creating an equal and just society. According to Robert, that society was socialism, which is a transition between capitalism and communism. Communism is a classless system of social organization in which the means of production are collectively owned and managed by the people (through the state,) but in which the coercive state has withered away, and citizens contribute to society according to their abilities and receive according to their needs. Economically cooperative and planning replaces the free market. Profits that come out of the work force go back into society. For example, education, health care, and other services are free to the public. By contrast, a capitalist society has an economic class structure of upper-class, wealthy owners who govern, followed by middle, lower, and under classes. The means of production are privately owned by individual capitalists and corporations, which reap large profits and increasing wealth for the owners. A free market economy of supply and demand determines whose needs are met or not met. People contribute according to the rewards they hope to get.

Even though Robert believed that socialism could create a just society, he was a born critic and he never held back if he detected wrongdoing. For instance, in January, 1982, Alan Katz wrote in the *Denver Magazine:* "Oddly, Trujillo admits that he'd be less partisan if he lived in the Soviet Union. He seems to enjoy the antagonistic relationship he has with society, saying if I lived in a socialist country, 'I would be willing to criticize whatever weaknesses I could detect.' Throughout his adult life Robert was an activist." He detested apathy, which he felt was an unnatural state of being. "Action" he said "is the law of nature. The natural process of nature," he said, "is aggressive, always moving forward." Thus, he was always working aggressively to educate people to achieve socialism. Many people socialized by those who profit from the status quo responded with suspicion, fear, and anger.

The old warrior Robert pushed and pushed until the end. He died as he lived, with tremendous courage and compassion. He told me near the end, "I could see why some people take their lives when they have this unbearable pain that I have, but" he added, "I could never do that to my family." He stood tall even in his last days. He was in control of his own life until a few days before he died of lung cancer. He lived 82 years, and he left his mark. This old communist left a big red contribution of Love.

Chapter 1

My story of Robert Trujillo

1942

I was conceived and born during wartime.
My nickname as a child was "Atomic Midget"
I am a volcano full of Love.
The lava is my passion of love; my life's purpose is
to learn my own lessons and to help bring peace to
myself, my family, and the world.

1944

When I was two, we moved into a big white house with two
stairways. One I ran up, the other one I ran down. I thought,
"Dios, va hacer gran vivir en esta casa tan vieja y grande." ("God,
it's going to be great living in this big old house.") My happiest memory is of the piano, and it helped make me a lifelong
romantic. It was there for Mom to play and sing to us kids.
"Orlanda loves a soldier, Rena loves a sailor, but Mary Lou
loves all the guys in the Marines." I loved everyone. That was
my essence.

On the other hand, I was so scared at times that I would
crawl into a small opening under the stairs. In the kitchen
there was a small door near the cellar stairs that hardly anyone
could notice. I went in there because I was afraid that the Ku
Klux Klan or the FBI would break into our home and kill my
Daddy. I didn't know why. Daddy was good; he was like

Christ to me. He took care of everything and helped everyone. One time he was unemployed for a long period of time, and a girlfriend asked me, "How do you and your family eat?" I replied, innocently, "Oh, Daddy takes care of us. He takes care of everyone." I didn't know who the Klan was, but I did know that they wore white sheets and burned and killed Blacks, Catholics, and Communists. And my father, Robert, was a communist all of my life with him.

How did it feel under the staircase? My past replays in stereo, Hi Fi, as vivid memories run through my mind. I have a flash-back, I'm in the hole again, asking, "Why do they want to kill my Daddy? What would I do if they did?" I feel alone and afraid, but I also feel safe in here, because if they come in the house and tried to kill us all, I'd run in here and they would never know. So I wouldn't die. And if they killed my Daddy and Mama and all my brothers and sisters, I would still be alive to carry on the struggle.

As a young child I felt that fear, but as an adolescent it dissipated as I became more analytical. As I matured, the things I had learned from my father came to fit reality. I experienced discrimination from some of my classmates because I was a poor Mexican American. I was super sensitive, and when they would look at me strangely, I knew they were talking about me. In addition, I had to conceal the fact that my father was a communist, because in school the teachers taught how bad communists were. But I was proud of him and proud of being a Mexican American. One time one of my older brothers told me, "You are so Mexican." I retorted, "Aren't you? He always tried to get me to assimilate, telling me to dress like Anglos and take on the customs of American society. My brother married a beautiful Anglo girl and felt he had to fit in. I did not. Furthermore, Mom made my clothes out of flour sacks, and I didn't dress like the other girls. One year Dad bought me a long blue coat that was way too big for me. But I loved it. He didn't have money to buy me a new coat every year. I wore it for a few years. He figured I'd grow into it. Today, people would think I was a gang member!

I turn now to the story of my father Robert Trujillo, which begins with his parents. I often wonder what his father would have thought of his only son, who survived American society as a communist. I recall that when my grandmother was dying, she was still praying for her only son, Robert, to return to the Catholic Church.

Robert Trujillo

*"The soul, which sees what is really good infallibly, desires
the good it has discerned."*

—*Socrates*

Robert's parents, Francisco and Marina.

Chama, Colorado, 1903

The red-hot coals from the kitchen stove warmed up the three-room adobe house in Chama, where the midwife was preparing for the delivery of Marina and Francisco's first child. Attached to the kitchen was the dining room/bedroom, where a loud cry came from the newborn baby boy, Robert Trujillo.

Marina's eyes filled with tears as she gave a sigh of relief when the midwife announced that the baby was alive and healthy. Marina had delivered a stillborn child a year before in 1902. So this birth of their first son was a blessing and a miracle.

Chama is a small town four miles east of San Luis, the oldest town in Colorado. San Luis was founded on June 21, 1851. After the Mexican war of 1848, the United States took possession of an area called the New Mexico Territory (now

Costilla County, Colorado). Historically, the San Luis Valley has been one of the poorest communities in the state. The San Luis Valley, comprising 8,000 square miles, is the world's largest alpine valley, surrounded by lush green fields at the foot of the Sangre de Cristo Mountains to the east. Slightly to the south and east of San Pedro Mesa are the Sanchez Reservoir and the Sanchez State Wildlife Area. To the west are the San Luis Hills with the San Juan Mountains. To the north is the Blanca Massif. Surrounding the valley in the summertime are beautiful green trees, colorful wild irises, milkweed, and sunflowers, framed by high, majestic mountains. Fresh clean air and the sound of roosters wake up the villagers before the sun rises. At night the stars shine like diamonds all around the deep dark sky. In the wintertime a cold breeze wakes the villagers in the early hours of the morning. Many families have coal or wood stoves, and a few still have outdoor toilets. In the wintertime the mountains surrounding the valley are snow-packed and look like the twin sisters of the pure white sands of Mount Blanca in the summertime. On a hilltop overlooking the town of San Luis is a path leading up to the Stations of the Cross. The original sculpture at each cross was hand-sculpted in 1990 by Huberto Maestas, a well-known San Luis artist, adding Catholic tradition and culture to the valley. The long winding path and beautification of the shrine at the top are maintained by devout townspeople. People passing through San Luis to get to Chama often stop to make the pilgrimage to Maestas' Stations of the Cross.

A clear river runs a few feet south of the main street in the tiny town of Chama. Chama has an old but well-maintained Catholic Church, a post office, and a small store. The school in recent years has deteriorated. Families still look out of their windows whenever a car drives down the main dirt road, because visitors are uncommon here. The sound of bees buzzing around the sunflowers and the perfumed scent of the wild flowers decorate the houses made of adobe. The villages of San Luis Valley resemble Indian Pueblos.

The majority of the people in the San Luis Valley are of Mexican descent, working class, poor, and Catholic. At the turn of the century, when Robert was born, a wealthy family owned the majority of the land in the valley. The division of class, race, labor, and culture was obvious. Robert's family, like most of the other families, was Mexican, poor, and deeply Catholic.

Robert's family consisted of his father, Francisco, his mother, Marina, who joined together in a marriage arranged by their parents. Robert had four sisters: Odila, Beatrice, Della, and Madeline. He had two baby brothers who died as infants. He said, "I had two brothers and four sisters. One baby brother died in 1902 before I was born, and the other baby brother died in 1904. The doctor claimed they were too sick and weak from malnutrition." In a Denver Post article in 1978 Richard Johnson illustrates Robert's stewing anger: "Memories of his two baby brothers who died from malnutrition clouded his mind and he felt the rage stir within him as he remembered his mother feeding them *poliadas*. Trujillo explained the term in a flinty tone, which suggested that he still feels outrage: 'It was a liquid made of water and wheat flour made into a thin paste, which we drank. We had potbellies. We were starving. I don't know why I survived.'"[1]

Della, Robert's sister, also spoke to me in a telephone conversation in 2002 of the loss of their two infant brothers and her mother's temperament:

> Our brother, Charles, died a baby, and another baby may have been born dead. Mother never talked to us about anything. We never got any hugging and kissing, no carino (affection). I guess they [Mother's generation] didn't expect any. Mother was cold. At that time maybe it was the culture. She sure had a temper. She would bend her fist and hit us kids with her knuckles. All we did was work like crazy.
>
> I might add Mother was very smart. She dug a deep hole in the dirt and placed layers of beets, turnips and other vegetables that had grown and she

---

[1]   *The Denver Post*, "Communist in Colorado", by Richard Johnson, February 19, 1978.

put layers of dirt on top of them. She dug so deep so [that] the soil would freeze and we had fresh vegetables all winter long. She was also good with herbs. We would get some herbs, take the roots off, tie them with twigs and hang them out to dry. People from the surrounding villages would come and get herbs from her.

Robert added to his sister's story of the situation of that time to me. "We were very poor. My father was a sheepherder, and his wages were fifteen dollars a month. He had to go three hundred miles away from his family for ten to eleven months out of the year. Mother, my little sisters, and I worked the six-acre farm raising some food while he was gone."

Robert's father was a Penitente, a member of a Catholic brotherhood in the Southwest.

Charles Sullivan wrote:

The Penitentes started back when there was no government, there was no church, and there was no school in this part of the country. The Penitentes, more than anyone, filled the administrative, religious, and cultural vacuum. They also provided great political service.[2]

The Penitentes also spilled their blood to ensure the abundance of crops, animals, and children. The practice was acceptable; in fact, the people for whom the Penitentes provided this service for revered them. It was a melding of Christian belief with very old pagan rituals.

My father defined the Penitentes during a 1976 radio interview with Bob Gordon, on KOA in Denver, Colorado.

---

[2]   Charles Sullivan. Here Is My Kingdom, *Hispanic-American Literature and Art For Young People.* (Harry N. Abrams, Incorporated, 1994.)

The Penitentes were a religious cult that was brought
in by the Catholic priests from Spain. They had a
committee of men called the Penitentes Club. [The
Penitentes were lay brothers, not ordained priests.]
The Penitentes used to whip themselves during
Lent (the Holy Week) and bleed. Lent goes from Ash
Wednesday through Good Friday and lasts forty
days. This ritual was practiced to punish themselves
for their sins. I have vivid memories of my father
whipping himself late at night to punish himself for
his sins. As Christ suffered for the sins of others, the
Penitentes performed similar self-sacrifices for the
good of the people. There was a church next door
to my mother's house we could see into the ceiling
where thousands of black blood stains shot up from
the Penitentes whipping themselves. My father was
a kind, loving, religious and disciplined man, who I
had a lot of respect for.

While Robert's father, Francisco, was gone, Robert was left
in charge of the family. "I was responsible for the care of the
small farm that my mother had inherited. When my father
returned home, he brought ribbons for my three little sisters."
Della, Robert's sister, referring to their father, said, "He came
home long enough to make a baby. Then he was gone again."

Robert loved and respected his mother dearly. He said,
"Mother was a strong, determined, disciplined, and deeply
religious woman. She was a healer and midwife. She was
called upon many times to deliver a baby for the villagers."

Della said, "They would give her a small bag of potatoes
or a few carrots, and my sisters and I would get so mad. We
would tell Mother that they were taking advantage of her.
But she wanted to help. They would come for her in a horse
and buggy in the middle of a cold winter night. Ignoring
our request, she kept on doing it." Robert was a serious and
responsible child. He told me:

I worked hard and seldom had time to play. When I
was seven years old, one of my chores was to irrigate

the crops of our small farm during the night. I had a lot of time to think, and this was when I started questioning everything about life. I was mainly concerned with the injustices that I saw all around me. I questioned why some people were born only to struggle and suffer, like my own family, while others were born to enjoy life and all their wealth. I saw that the bosses lived in beautiful homes and did not seem to work at all, while the poor Mexicans worked long hours and barely made a living.

Robert vented his frustration at times in destructive ways. He shared with me a story of his behavior.

When I was quite young, my mother would ask me to chase the chickens off the roof of our adobe house. I got tired of having to do all my chores. Having to chase the chickens off the roof every day just added fuel to my anger. So one day I climbed the roof and broke the legs of the chickens with a big rock. I rationalized that my job would be easier because now the chickens would not be able to climb back up again. I was not very proud of my behavior because I knew it was wrong, but I rebelled, taking out my frustration on the poor chickens.

As a young boy Robert said, "School was a great joy for me and learning gave meaning to my life. I loved learning. I was a bright student, curious, creative, and I guess they would have labeled me as gifted in the area of critical thinking. I earned high grades and won many spelling contests, even when I would compete against the older students." His beautiful handwriting and his grammar were close to perfect.

Robert had a pinto horse that he rode to run errands for his family. His younger sisters were not allowed to ride it because, as his sister, Della, said, "It belonged to him because he was the one in charge when our father was gone. He was very strict with us girls. At times he even hit us." Robert's sisters were beautiful teenagers. Della said, "Brother,' [as his sisters called him] watched over us in a protective and, at times, extremely stem manner."

When Robert was sixteen, his father became ill. Robert said,

> For three days before my father, Francisco, died of tuberculosis, me and my family watched our father lose his mind as he mumbled words of despair over having to leave me, his oldest son, with all the responsibility of supporting my mother and his four daughters. Odila was twelve years old, Beatrice was eleven years old, Della was seven years old, and Madeline was only three years old when our father died.
>
> Della recalled her father's death: "The coffin was hand made from flat boards, and it had black satin material. I remember my dad just lying there."

Robert shared with me how heartbroken and scared he was after the loss of his father.

> When my father passed away in 1919, there was no pension for widows, their children, or those in need. Social Security and unemployment insurance was unknown. My mother was left with a small plot of land, on which she raised beans, one or two pigs, and nothing more. She would wear her shoes down to nothing, and then she was barefooted. There was no possibility at all for new shoes. Our clothes came from flour sacks. These too were mended over and over again. Money was a completely foreign commodity to us. I was forced to quit school and get a job to save our house and land. I was very young, and I was head of our household. I had to be strong even though I was all scared and torn up inside.
>
> Three days after my father died, three people came to ask my mother for the money in the treasury. My father was the treasurer and bookkeeper for the Penitentes. Since he was never home, Mother was in charge of the money. She started to cry and used the

end of her apron, trembling, to wipe her tears. She had no money. They wanted $190.00 she had taken and already spent. When she opened the cigar box where she kept the money, there was hardly any. So they made her sign three notes, and she put up the few acres of land and our home for collateral until I was able to pay the missing money back.

Robert's father left a $500.00 debt, and the family needed money. With no other choice and a lot of pain and frustration over having to quit school in the 8th grade, Robert accepted his role as the man of the house and went with his uncle to Nebraska to pick sugar beets for ten cents an hour. The little money he made he sent home to his family.

Less than a year after the death of his father, Robert faced another heartbreaking loss. "After my father died at the age of forty two, less than a year later my twelve-year old sister, Beatrice, died of tuberculosis." They did not have any money for doctors and medical care, and another one of his loved ones was taken from him. Della was eight when Beatrice was dying, and she remembered,

> Beatrice was very beautiful. She had big brown eyes, and she was very quiet. She never got into trouble like we did. And when she was real sick, I went next door and stole a pear from our aunt's orchard. We were very envious because they had a fruit orchard and we did not. Anyway, I didn't have any brains and I went into her place and took it. It was in the autumn. I remember because the pear was still green. I took the pear to her bed, and I whispered, "Beatrice, I brought you a pear," and she said, softly, "Put it under my pillow." " She died that night.

Robert, who was seventeen at the time, took another job, as a sheepherder. Only a few heard his cries of grief for his father and little sister as they echoed along the canyon walls where he tended the sheep. "I felt that my whole world caved in on me, my whole family was broken-hearted and nothing would ever be the same again. Before my father died, even though we were gravely poor, we were family and we had our father and now we only had each other. I was not only overwhelmed with grief, I was angry." His entire life seemed to be motivated by anger and personal suffering, and so he empathized with the suffering of others. For seven years Robert supported his family. Della said, "We seldom ever saw Brother after he left on that train to tend sheep with our cousin."

Robert on the train, on the right.

Robert's mother, Marina, was widowed for six years, remarrying in 1924. "I was twenty-one when my mother married Patricio Valdez," Robert said, "and I went to work in the Pitkin Coal Mines for two years, making fifty cents an hour. Even then a conclusion was impressed indelibly upon my consciousness: Men who didn't work were getting rich from the agony of those of us who crawled into dark, wet tunnels and choked on coal dust."

Robert continued, "Me and my sisters took to our new stepfather, but he, like our father, was gone away working a good deal of the time. Frances, a daughter, was born to my mother and Patricio. Patricio also had a son, Manuel, and two daughters, Cerrila and Josefita, from a previous marriage. I grew to love my stepfather and remember him fondly as being very good to us. Patricio died nine years later, in 1933."

"I was still supporting my family when I fell in love and married Eduvijen (Edna) Sanchez in 1926. I was twenty-three, and Edna was sixteen when we married." Robert said, "She was beautiful, with pale skin, curly, auburn hair, and a look of innocence." Edna had been born on March 9, 1910. Her family was of Mexican-American descent, working class, and poor. They were Catholic and spoke only Spanish. Her mother had died when Edna was a year-and-a-half, and her nine-year-old sister, Reina, became her mother figure. Their father, Pete Sanchez, was left to raise Edna, her sister, and one brother. (One sister had died giving birth). Shortly after the loss of his first wife, Pete married Raquel. Edna and her siblings did not receive much nurturing from their stepmother because she was always outdoors working like a man.

I recall that when I was a child, my step-grandmother, Raquel, looked and acted just like a man. She had crossed eyes and short hair and dressed in men's clothing. I once heard a story about how Raquel looked so much like a man that when she went into a women's restroom in a public place, she almost got arrested because they thought she was a man!

In an interview story for a Chicano/Chicana Studies class, my sister-in-law Julie described Edna's childhood and the way she was raised:

Edna was the youngest child and the only child left at home alone. Her family moved around a lot because they were migrant farm workers. Her dad and stepmother also worked in a timber area hauling logs from the mountains to make railroad ties. Little Edna would take care of their house and the animals while her parents were gone. At times they left her without food and, due to that, throughout her life she was afraid of being left alone. She liked going to her older sister's house because her sister always fed her, and Edna remembered her as being very good to her. Edna was taken out of school when her parents had to work far away from home. Besides, the classes were all taught in English and it was very difficult for her to learn a foreign language.

Edna, my mom shared with me an episode in school that had traumatized her. "The nuns hit me because I would not speak in English. I didn't know English. So my father took me out of school in the third grade because of this incident, and my education ended." As an adult she developed great reading skills, and she read and understood college material.

Julie continued the interview:

When Edna married Robert, the priest instructed Edna to always obey her husband and to have many children, warning her it was a sin to prevent having children. Because of this command, Edna and Robert had six children when they lived in Walsenburg. They later had three more children. She [Edna] had a hysterectomy and couldn't have any more children. Julie added, "She really took to heart the command of the Catholic priest.

Edna lived much of her life in a world of dreams. Many times she talked to me about the beautiful love she and Robert shared and about all the dreams they had for a better life for their children. She said, "Roberto was my love, my teacher, and my caretaker. I was fifteen when I fell in love with him. He always took care of me. When we were going together, I was making homemade soap once with lye, and I got burned real bad, and he took me to the doctor. He was the one who took care of things ever since we fell in love." She showed me the white scars on her hands and arms from the burns.

Robert shared with me, "I got married making fifty cents an hour, and then we moved to Walsenburg for a job in the local coal mines." Robert was not a romantic like Edna. He used to say, "A man's hard work, day in and day out, is proof of a man's love for his wife and his children." Then the Great Depression hit and affected Robert's ability to support his family.

When the black cloud of the Depression hit, the whole nation went into turmoil. The final blow for Robert was when he showed up for work in 1929 and was told he no longer had a job! If Robert's strength and ability to survive were tested in his youth, the struggles of the next decade would be his supreme test.

Chapter 2

The Great Depression (1929–1940)

1929

The Depression in 1929 had devastating effects on people throughout the country. Robert was one of the millions of Americans thrown out of work. It was the most severe depression ever seen in the history of world capitalism.

Everything came to a standstill. The stock market was in a shambles. The closing of banks and the collapse of America's financial infrastructure threw the whole country into chaos.[3]

Despair, hunger, and misery plagued the nation. Farmers lost their farms, and evictions became the norm. Some of the wealthy lost everything in the stock market. Individuals and private organizations like churches did what they could and were able to help some, but among the masses, hunger spread all across the land: to the cotton fields of the South, the steel

---

[3]   The Wall Street crash on Black Thursday, October 24, 1929 brought an end to the Roaring Twenties. Large and small businesses failed. Farmers along with many others were forced into bankruptcy. Production in the United States fell by more than fifty percent. Automobile production in April of 1929 stood at a high of 621,910 cars per month. By December of that year production had plummeted to 119,950 cars per month. Declines hit basic industries throughout the nation. Cuts in wages decreased membership of the American Federation of Labor (AFL) because workers no longer had money to pay union dues.

towns of the Midwest, and the coal mines in the Southwest where Robert worked to feed his growing family.

Walsenburg, Colorado 1930

With sweat rolling down her face, Edna continued wetting and sweeping the dirt floors when she was surprised by the tone of Robert's voice. "I have to leave! There are no jobs here." "Where are you going?" Edna asked. " I'm going to Albuquerque, New Mexico. There has to be some work there." Edna burst out in tears and ran into his arms. "You can't go! I'm afraid for you, for me, for the kids." In a shaky voice Robert said,

"I'm afraid too, but we will starve if I don't go and find work." That was the end of the conversation. Robert went out back, grabbed a rooster, killed it, and took it into the house. Edna didn't say a word. She cleaned the bird, cut it up, fried it, and packed it in a shoebox.

Robert gathered a few belongings and a statue of Jesus Christ. While he was employed at the coal mine, he bought two statues, one of Jesus Christ and one of the Virgin Mary, which he had given to his mother. These were his family's most sacred possessions. He gently wrapped the one statue in a brown bag, being careful not to break it. He was thinking that he would sell it for food. He hugged his three crying children and held his wife close to his heart, telling her not to worry. Off he went to the freight trains to start his life as a hobo. He jumped into the boxcar with the help of two men who had just jumped in. Several men looking sad, depressed, and hopeless greeted him. There were some 30 men in the boxcar. Robert shared his fried chicken with a few of the men as they each shared their stories and found that they were all in similar situations. He said,

> It was getting dark that evening when we arrived in New Mexico. I got off the train, and as I was walking with my statue under my arm, a guard approached me. He demanded to know what I had in the package. I told him, I have Jesus Christ in the package. The guard said, laughing at me, "You're a damn

fool! Jesus Christ is in heaven," and he made me unwrap it. I said, "Look, I have his picture here." I was not well educated, and I didn't know the difference between a statue and a picture. He told me, "You are never to come into this railroad camp again and if you ever do, I'll throw your ass in jail."

Robert fell into a few part-time jobs, including working in a junkyard, but none of them paid enough for him to stay in Albuquerque. So he returned to Walsenberg to his family after a few months.

I managed to save a little money, to put gas in my old pickup truck that was parked for months, because I had no money for gas. I went to the coal mine and started putting pieces of coal in my truck. When I had about half a ton of coal, a guard came over to me and put a gun to my chest. He told me, "You put that coal back, or I'll throw you in jail." Of course, I put it all back. I was so upset, I wrote a letter to President Roosevelt telling him of my situation and all the problems I was having. A short time later a lady from the Red Cross came to me with a copy of the letter I had written the President. She asked me if I had written it. I saw my handwriting and told her yes I had. After that incident they started giving me milk, bread, and other food products. Before that, all we were getting was 25 pounds of flour for a whole month.

Still seeking work, Robert went to his priest in complete desperation, begging him to give him some kind of work, cutting the lawn or whatever work he could give. "He turned me down and told me to pray and be patient. I left demoralized, thinking I need help right now!"

Radio announcer Bob Gordon asked Robert about his experience during the Depression:

Bob Gordon: You are a member of a political organization that has gone through a lot in terms of the political heritage

*Robert Edna and the four older children during the depression,
Ruth on Robert's lap, Pete on Edna's lap, Frank on the
left and Fred on the right.*

of the United States, especially in the later portion of the 20th
century. Why don't you tell us something about your involvement with this political organization?

Robert: I didn't know anything about the Communist Party of the United States. I was a coal miner

at the time, around the neighborhood of of Walsenburg, Colorado. I was raising a large family. All of a
sudden I found out that people were being laid off in
Walsenburg and throughout the nation, and finally
it came to the moment where I was laid off of my job
in the coal mine. Then we began to struggle for the
right to our lives and the right to a job, and before
I knew it, I was getting literature from the National
Unemployment Council. And through their newspaper I found articles about the Communist Party
of the United States. This was the first time I heard
about the Communist Party.[4,5]

On July 4, 1930, the Trade Union Unity League organized
a national conference in Chicago to bring together the unemployed across the nation. That conference led to the founding of National Unemployment Organization, which created
councils to address the various problems the unemployed
were facing.

The Depression lasted well over a decade, with thousands
upon thousands continuing their unsuccessful search for work.
When the crisis began, one-sixth of the population (917,000
people) was jobless. In 1932 a quarter of the work force, or
13 million American people, were unemployed. In 1933 more
than half of the steel-mill workers across the country were
unemployed, and many of those who remained employed
were cut back to part-time work.

---

[4] The Communist Party in the United States was established
in Chicago in 1919, deriving from the Socialist Party that
had formed in 1900. World War I, along with the proletarian
revolution in Russia, establishing the first Communist state,
had a great impact on workers in the United States. Many
workers in the United States, struggling from the economic
collapse of the Depression, identified with the Russian
workers. After the Depression millions of workers, modeling
the Communist Soviet Union, joined the Communist Party.

[5] Excerpts of Robert's interview in 1976, with KOA-Radio
announcer, Bob Gordon.

Labor Historian Philip Foner noted that Black workers felt the seriousness of the crisis four years before the Depression. Blacks have always been the last to be hired and the first to be fired. Foner goes on to say, "In the early months of 1929, with the economy supposedly flourishing as never before, 300,000 Black industrial workers, about one-fifth of all Blacks employed in industry, had already been thrown out of work."

The Depression eventually affected everyone, but in the beginning it affected the jobs held mainly by Blacks, Mexicans, and other people of color.[6]

I asked Robert whether he ever in his life had hit a breaking point. He replied,

> During the time when I was out of work, our babies would keep my wife and I up half the night crying. Because my wife was so sick, I would help her with the care of the babies. We had five of them at that time. I would be up walking the floor rocking one of the little ones to sleep so that she could get some rest. I don't know why they cried so much. Maybe they were hungry? And after I returned to bed, insomnia set in. I was so worried and fearful about how I was going to feed and care for my family.

Robert shared with me a recurring dream that had plagued him for as long as he could remember. "In the dream I was pushing a wheelbarrow, and I was so excited because it was full of food. I was pushing it, rushing home to take the food to my family. But when I arrived at my house, I went to get the food, and it had all turned into rocks. I would awaken perspiring because it upset me so damn much!"

Robert decided to stand up and fight for his survival. He went to a gathering of many desperate families, where he got up to speak. He started by saying, "We either unite and struggle

---

6   Foner, Philip S. *Organized Labor and the Black Worker 1619–1973.* (New York: Praeger, 1974.) *cited in Highlights of A fighting History, 60 Years of the Communist Party USA* (International Publishers, New York, 1979, p. 53.)

together to demand jobs and food, or we will all starve." After he finished his speech, he passed out from pure anger and fear. "But," he said, "I got up." And from that day forward, his direction in life was clear. He chose to be the responsible man. He was not only responsible for his own family; he took on as well the social/political responsibility for helping others.

On a cold, freezing winter night, Robert and several men jumped the fence of the coal mine to steal coal, knowing they were breaking the law and they could be caught. But they needed to feed and provide heat for their families. Others who felt the pressures too great survived by escaping: some walked out on their families, and some turned to drinking. Yet many were hard-working Christians, who believed in doing things the right way. So, along with Robert, they started to move in the direction of political unity and struggle.

The hard times were affecting people everywhere around the nation; farmers demanding some action during the crisis turned to demonstrations, and violence erupted. They were desperate because they were losing their farms to the banks that held their mortgages. As evictions took hold, many farmers as well as the Black cotton workers left the South and moved to Chicago and to other cities and states in search of work. Across the country a great migration began as people pulled up stakes and moved from place to place trying to survive.

At the same time, as hunger increased around the nation, movements and organizations arose demanding jobs. Soup kitchens were formed and shanty towns called Hoovervilles sprang up in cities around the country. In April of 1936 three left-wing organizations, the Unemployment Councils, the Unemployment Leagues, and the Workers Alliance of America, met in Washington, D. C. They joined forces and formed the Unity Convention. This is when Robert became Colorado's State Chairman of the Workers Alliance of America.

As the State Chairman for the Workers Alliance of America in the 1930s, Robert, along with others, worked to exert political pressure. One of the programs that came out of their efforts was the Works Project Administration (WPA), along with other programs of relief, recovery, and reform that were responses to the Great Depression. The people continued to organize on a large scale.

Organizations mushroomed to mobilize against hunger and to demand jobs. Seeing the need, Robert became an organizer and a leader of the people struggling to find jobs in Walsenburg, Colorado. His credentials were: an eighth-grade education, strong values from his family, the teachings of Christ, and a passion for protecting and providing not only for his own family but also for the men, women, and children suffering just like him. Robert's oldest son, Frank, and eldest daughter, Ruth, shared memories of their life growing up during the Depression. Frank shared reflections on that period:

> I am the eldest offspring of the nine children born to Robert and Eduvijen Trujillo. I was born in Chama, Colorado, on September 5, 1927. I was baptized and named Francisco Demetrio Trujillo, after my paternal grandfather.
>
> The early memories I have of my father are that he was a hard worker (when he could find work) and he was always helping other people to unite and work together for a better life. As a child in Walsenburg, Colorado, I remember all we had was a radio, and every morning my father listened to the early morning news while he had his breakfast. The first organization he [helped] form in the early thirties was the Workers' Alliance, a group of, maybe, twenty-four people who worked together to fight for jobs and relief, as they called it in those days. I remember at age six learning and singing a union song. I would stand on a chair and sing to the group. This song was sung to the tune of "The Battle Hymn of the Republic:
>
> (Chorus)
> Companieros a La Lucha
> Companieros a La Lucha
> Companieros a La Lucha
> A La Lucha hasta veneer.

(Chorus)
Comrades onward to the fight
Comrades onward to the fight
Comrades onward to the fight
To the fight until we win.

The workers have learned their lesson.
They know who their enemies are, and that is why
they will fight and fight to form one union.

(Chorus)

[Frank continued:] "In the late thirties Dad was
thrown in jail for parading in the streets without a
permit. They were demanding jobs, clothing, and
relief for the poor. He was also jailed in Trinidad,
Colorado, in 1939 for marching in the streets. He
was also jailed in Washington D.C. in 1938, but I
don't remember for what.

In the 1930s my father worked in the coal mine two
or three days a month. I recall him asking a county
commissioner who owned three coal mines in Huerfano County for more work. The commissioner told
him he had a job offer as a truck driver at $44.00 a
month. But he added that there was one condition
and that was that my father keep his mouth shut
and quit organizing people. My father did not get
the job because his devotion was to people and he
would not stop organizing them.

Ruth, our oldest sister, carried a tremendous amount of
responsibility because our mother was frequently sick. Ruth
was like a second mother to all of us children. She shared stories of her life growing up during the Depression.

I was born in 1928. A year later we had a Depression. It seems like it was forever. Everyone was
poor. Our neighbors were Yugoslavian. We taught
them Spanish, and they taught us Slovenian. Mrs.

Radovich baked the best French bread in the world. She taught Mom how to make it, and they loved Mom's tortillas. Four years ago I looked for and found Helen, "Che Che," Mrs. Radovich's daughter. We hadn't seen each other since we were children. She told me, "If it had not been for your dad, we would have starved. He would go to Chama, Colorado, and, since some of his relatives were farmers, they would give him beans and potatoes etc., and he would always give us some." Ruth added that Che Che's father had been killed in a mine accident. I remember Mary Radovich, her eyes real big, telling us about the accident. I remember the day he was buried.

As a small child in Walsenburg [Ruth continued] I walked into Mom and Dad's bedroom. They were lying in bed, fully clothed, singing "Una Noche Serena y Occura" ("One Night Serene and Dark"). That scene has been in my heart and head forever. Mom loved to sing, and she had a beautiful voice. I asked her where she had learned to sing those Mexican love songs, religious songs, and revolutionary songs. She said her aunt Luz played the organ and taught her the music. Mom, in turn, taught the songs to us. She used to break out singing, and we would all join in and harmonize.

Ruth shared some of her happy childhood memories during the Depression.

Living in Walsenburg, Colorado, for the first years of our lives, was great when we visited our grandmother and many relatives in the San Luis Valley. Chama was our second home and there was a lot of love and fellowship. Mom and Dad and the latest baby sat in front and us kids in the back. Fred grew up to be much bigger than I. (They all did), but Freddy sat on my lap and he had the boniest butt in the whole world. I was very glad to finally arrive. We would stop at Mom's sister's house, Tio Andres and Tia Leonarda, who lived about a block from Grandma. We would visit awhile, and then us kids would ask when we were we going to Chama. Grandma's house was in Chama. But Mom and Dad took us to see as many relatives as we could.

Once we went to see Tio Elario, Mom's uncle. He was a midget. Pete, my baby brother, was about three, and we all sat very quietly because we had never seen Tio Elario before. He glared at us and especially Pete. (I heard later that he didn't like kids very much). Anyway, he got off his chair, grabbed his cane and yelled at Pete and said in Spanish, *'Que estas mirando, nino loco?'* ('What are you looking at, you crazy kid?') Pete screamed and ran out the door. Poor Pete. When I looked at him, he was very pale, and it took us a while to find him. We never wanted to go there again.

All of Robert's children were brought up with a basic understanding of Catholicism and politics. The main values were thou shalt not kill, equality and justice for all, sharing, and serving and caring about the welfare of others. In 1967 reporter Leonard Larson interviewed Robert and asked him about his stance on the Catholic Church.

Larsen: I suppose you were raised a Catholic. Did you leave the church then?

Robert: My wife and I would go to church every Sunday, and the priest told us we shouldn't even steal coal at night to warm our houses and heat some food if we had a few pinto beans to cook. I was not mad at the church; I was mad at the preaching of an individual priest. We had another priest in Walsenberg who came to our meetings and spoke in favor of our programs.

Larsen: Do you attend church now? Robert: No, I don't go to any churches. I don't see any reason for it. When they tell me that it's God's will if you're poor or it's God's will if you're a millionaire, I don't agree with that. It's not true. It's not God's will that we should be poor or that others should be million-aires... I go [to church] if there's a wedding or a funeral, but I don't go to church regularly. But you don't see me in beer joints either; you don't see me in trouble with the police for getting drunk.

Larsen: Robert are you an atheist?

Robert: The Communist Party does not force me to believe whatever they say. I can believe what-ever I want. I am one hundred percent Christian. I don't have to go to church to be a Christian, and I don't have to get down on my knees and pray to the Almighty. I think I can please Him [God] more by doing what's right in this world. This is what Jesus fought for. This is why He was crucified.

Larsen: On a wall of Robert's house is a news-paper picture, a clipping of a Denver priest of Our Lady of Guadalupe Church, who has become known as something of a maverick in the Catholic Church. What Trujillo particularly liked in the news-paper portrait of Father Lara were the priest's con-clusions that prayers alone will never free the poor and oppressed and that it is unrealistic to expect to help the poor without political action.[7]

When the oppressed in Walsenburg united, they had meet-ings and public demonstrations. Robert played a leading role. He and his followers demanded basic necessities such as jobs, food, beds, and respect for their demands. Out of this pressure the government responded with the Works Project Administration (W.P.A.). It was formed to assume a dominant role in work relief activities that helped the unem-ployed. A telling incident took place when the Huerfano

---

[7]   Excerpts from an interview, Larsen, "Denver Communist 'Struggles On" *The Denver Post.* October 15, 1967.

county commissioners in Walsenburg, Colorado, answered a plea from the people for mattresses. The county commissioners sent a truckload of soiled mattresses from the Veterans' Hospital to answer the plea of the people. The people were outraged. They took a urine-soiled mattress and carried it with two long poles and marched to the courthouse. They took all the mattresses and displayed them in front of the city and county Court House with a huge sign that read: "We Are Not Animals, And We Are Bringing These Soiled Mattresses For The Officials Of The City To Sleep On. They Are Not Good Enough For The Workers Who Produce Everything In This Country."

Robert often talked to me about the Depression years and his reasons for becoming an activist. "With the 1929 Depression I found myself without a job, along with some twenty million other Americans. That condition lasted for a long time, and poor people everywhere were beginning to organize. I became interested and then active in the organizational [aspect of the struggle] and, as a consequence, was thrown into jail in Trinidad, Colorado, in 1939." He continued,

> While I was in jail in 1940, one of my daughters was born. I thought it unjust to find myself in jail. I had not committed any crime. I had not abused anyone. I had not resorted to stealing, [accept when he stold coal] nor did I do anything wrong or illegal. Others like me were also arrested simply because we were demanding the right to a job.
>
> Frank and Fred, Robert's sons, were told by our mother to hurry down to the jail and tell Robert that she was in labor. Fred recalls, "I was ten years old, and Frank was thirteen, and we walked almost running about a mile and a half to the jail. The jail was right behind the courthouse, and we were led inside. It was a dark dungeon, and then we stood in front of iron bars, and a huge lock where Dad was. We gave Dad the message, then we were quickly escorted out and hurried back home, to tell Mom about the horrible dark place Dad was in."

Robert continued,

> As a result of our struggles in the unemployment
> movement during the 1930's, we did manage to win
> some victories. Our struggles, along with efforts
> of other Socialists and people in other parts of the
> country, influenced the beginning of state and fed-
> eral social programs, which included a welfare sys-
> tem and public works. These programs of the U.S.
> Government were not a kind hand out from the gov-
> ernment. They came about from the efforts of many
> people demanding help so that we would not starve.

Being an activist for social change and justice was often
dangerous. Robert read and was angered by how many people like himself were incarcerated. For example, an incident
that affected him took place in July of 1932, when some 17,000
World War I veterans marched on Washington D.C. The veterans demanded payment of a bonus for their services during the
war. They were not supposed to receive the bonus until 1945,
but, with the Depression going on, they wanted their money at
that time. They built shacks and camped out near the Capitol.
Congress refused to honor their request, and some 2,000 veterans gave up and left. President Hoover and Congress feared
that the remaining veterans, called the Bonus Army, might
cause problems. Several veterans were killed when soldiers
led by General Douglas Macarthur dispersed the veterans and
destroyed the camps. The Bonus Army incident turned many
Americans against President Hoover.

Robert continued, "During this period my interest in organizing workers grew. I felt the enforced segregation of Mexican
people at our neighborhood theater as well as the low wages
were unfair. So I spoke out against these issues and tried to
educate the people to stand up to these unfair practices. The
authorities threatened to throw me in jail for this. I stood my
ground and received a lot of publicity from the newspapers."

Another incident that influenced Robert to stick to the Party
took place in Chicago. In 1937 police tried to stop a march,
opening fire on steel workers and killing ten people as they

marched toward Republic Steel because the steel company had refused to recognize the steelworkers' organizing committee. This was called the Memorial Day Massacre.

Even as a member and leader of the Communist Party, Robert had faults, and not all of his children agreed with him. At times relationships were strained, my older siblings were at times mistreated badly, as Robert's father had mistreated him, whereas the younger children were not, but we all loved him. He earned the respect of his wife and his children. No matter what challenges we each encountered, we respected the fact that he lived his beliefs. As his grandson said at the tribute honoring the Trujillo's life together, "Grandpa had more courage than any of us ever had." Robert was committed to his values, but we all experienced some suffering for his commitment to being a communist. Yet we give him credit as he did it his way. During his last interview, Robert was asked by University of Colorado Professor Michael S. Curnmings, "Do you have any regrets about your life?" Robert replied, "No, I think I did the right thing."

Many people did not feel that Robert and other communists did the right thing. The capitalist elites were disturbed because the people were rising in protest and resistance in astonishing numbers. By the 1940s many of the opponents of radicals began to worry about communists; a broad-ranging anti-Communist movement developed and started a national crusade against domestic communism.

The true test of Robert's commitment to the building of socialism came during the McCarthy period. If he was ever to let go of his struggle for justice, it would have been during this period when the pressure was on. But he didn't fold under the pressure.

Chapter 3

The McCarthy Period (late 1940s to late 1950s)

According to Robert, "The government passed laws against communists to defend the United States against the growing interest and involvement of the people with leftist organizations such as the Communist Party." These laws were created even before McCarthy's emergence and were then implemented at a crucial time in history when thousands of people were jobless and the Communist Party's influence was gaining ground.

Many of the organizations created during the Depression continued to be active in struggles involving labor unions and the Communist Party years later. Robert was one of the leaders who were educating the people about the causes of their unemployment. Workers learned about the class system in the U.S., and for some of them their worldview changed as to why they were victims of the economic crash. The McCarthy Era occurred in part as a result of this awakening of many people.[8]

---

[8]   In 1950, Joseph McCarthy was barely noticed in the U.S. Senate when he told a meeting of the Republican Women's Club that he had a large list [unsubstantiated] of "known Communists" who were at the time employed by the State Department. Over the next several years, he repeated sweeping charges against "subversives" in government, always without proof. He generated a chilling atmosphere of intimidation and stimulated unrestrained "Red" baiting and witch-hunting.

The Smith Act had been passed in 1940, making it illegal to support the violent overthrow of the U.S. government or to belong to any group that advocated this practice.

[See the Smith Act in the Appendix, page 163.]

Discussing the Smith Act, Pat Bell-Blau, a leader in the Communist Party for almost fifty years, wrote:

> But as everyone then began asking, what under the sun was the Smith Act? It was and is a short statute tucked away in a much longer law called the Alien Registration Act, adopted in the summer of 1940, when the nation was preparing to go to war. Its chief proponent was Rep. Howard Smith (D-VA), the Jesse Helms of his day.
>
> Rep. Smith's amendments made it a felony to "teach and advocate the necessity of overthrowing the government by force and violence." To comply with a later court decision, after the Act had received a test, the words were added, "as speedily as circumstances will permit." Prison sentences of up to five years were authorized and, by later amendment, the maximum penalty was increased to 10 years.
>
> The Act was not used until after the United States had entered World War II, when it was invoked to prosecute a number of Minnesota citizens opposed to the war, as members of the Socialist Workers' Party. It was then said that, if anything in the world was sacred to President Franklin Roosevelt, it was the war against the Fascist Axis. After that, the Smith Act was not heard of again until 1948, when it was made part of the government's avowed campaign to destroy the Communist Party.

In all of my exposure to the Communist Party not once do I recall anyone advocating the violent overthrow of the government. In fact the Communist Party platform nowhere advocated violence.

Limiting freedom of speech was the other purpose of the Smith Act, according to Dr. Herbert Aptheker in his book *Dare We Be Free?* The government in its interpretation effectively restricted the democratic rights of people." Aptheker points out:

> Zechariah Chafee Jr., Harvard Law School's and the nation's leading authority on the law of civil rights and civil liberties, failed at the time of the passage to note that the Smith Act's "other purposes" were most important. Chafee wrote, "Not until months later did I realize that the statute contains the most drastic restriction on freedom of speech ever enacted in the United States during peace."[9]

Twelve top leaders of the Communist Party of the United States were indicted in 1948. They were Eugene Dennis (General Secretary of the Party), William Z. Foster, Henry Winston, John Williamson, Benjamin J. Davis, Irving Potash, John Gates, Gus Hall, Gilbert Green, Carl Winters, Jacob Stachel, and Robert G. Thompson. All of them, with the exception of William Z. Foster, who was severed from the case due to illness, served long sentences. Henry Winston, a Black leader, went blind in prison because he did not receive proper care. He said, "They have taken away my sight, but they cannot take away my vision." Henry Winston and Gus Hall were very close to my father, and I enjoyed their visits.

Prior to the McCarthy Era, the U.S. government enforced several laws to suppress people who organized against it. The Taft-Hartley Act enacted in 1947 is a United States federal law that monitors the activities and power of labor unions. The law required officers of trade unions to file non-communist affidavits. President Truman used the Taft-Hartley Act to throw communists out of unions. And in 1950, as the Cold War intensified, another piece of legislation that effectively allowed the prosecution of members of the Communist Party,

---

[9]   *Hightlights of a Fighting History; 60 Years of the Communist Party USA.* (New York: International Publishers, 1979.)

was the Internal Security Act, also known as the McCarran Act. Congress passed the McCarran Act on September 23, 1950, requiring that, all communist groups had to register with the Attorney General. The act also prevented communists from entering the country. In addition, the President could jail subversives who secretly worked inside the country to overthrow the government—*in a national emergency*. What constitutes "a national emergency" was not defined in the McCarran Act. The act also prohibited all members of the Communist Party from being employed in or holding office in labor unions.

A career Foreign Service officer, George F. Kennan, formulated the policy of "containment" for fighting the Cold War (1947–1989) with the Soviet Union. This policy, blocking the expansion of Soviet influence, remained the basic strategy of the United States and became the basis of the Truman administration's foreign policy. The "X-file" article advocated "a long-term, patient, but firm and vigilant containment of Russian expansive tendencies." It proclaimed that a defeat of free institutions anywhere is a defeat everywhere. After the signing of the peace treaties in 1947, the alliance between the Soviet Union and the United States broke down, culminating in an ideological and political confrontation between the East and the West, which lasted throughout the Cold War period. During this period, the two superpowers formed separate military and political alliances, NATO, the pro-Western North Atlantic Treaty Organization and the pro-Soviet Warsaw Pact.

To these alliances and the foreign policy of "containment" by the Truman administration, Robert added a domestic component: "The leadership of the Party, along with others, was organizing the workers in the unions, demanding jobs and always struggling against racism. The laws against communists were a way of trying to stop the Party from gaining support." He added,

> Many of the leaders of the Party had to go underground, and many others were thrown in prison. Many were fired from their jobs to discourage them from participating in the Party. People were fired

from their jobs even if they were suspected of being communists. Many people from all walks of life were accused of being communists just for being seen at a meeting or being with a friend who may have been a sympathizer. Furthermore, many people were also blacklisted even though they weren't communists.

Throughout this repressive period, the Communist Party operated under tremendous pressure. But the anti-Red hysteria did not stop the Party from moving forward. An unintended result may have come out of this period altering the Party's influence and popularity, as some people became sympathetic towards communism. For instance, some in the movie industry came forward to help the accused when the government cracked down on actors and others.

I recall when I was a child hearing about the House Committee on Un-American Activities blacklisting anyone who had leftist affiliations. The Un-American Activities Committee claimed that the United States was being threatened by communist influences in the movie industry. The committee alleged that progressive statements and illustrations in the movies threatened the government, portraying some movies as communist propaganda. For example, in the 1947 movie "It's a Wonderful Life," statements were made such as, ["Share and share alike," which protagonist Peter Bailey yelled out to the greedy banker] "It's been twenty-five years since he [my father] and Uncle Billy started this business. I agree with you, he was not a businessman. He was a man of high ideals. He had strong character, never once thought of himself. He helped people come out of their slums. People were human beings to my father, and to you they are cattle."

Later in the movie, Bailey appealed to a panicky crowd that was trying to withdraw their money from the bank: "We've got to stick together, we've got to have faith in each other." All of these comments featured camaraderie and values of cooperation, not communist propaganda.

This fear tactic of redbaiting made many actors afraid of being harassed. "The unfriendly ten," a group of actors and others in the movie industry who were accused of being communists, turned to the Hollywood community for support. Many actors, producers, and screenwriters came to their defense. Hearings on communism in Hollywood were conducted to defend "the unfriendly ten." All of "the unfriendly ten" went to prison for six months to a year. The anti-Communist fever resulted in the House Un-American Activities Committee blacklisting six thousand individuals! This was in 1947 during the time of Cold War politics and the Truman administration.

Among those who were affected by the "Red Scare" that intensified the McCarthy hysteria were Robert and his family living in north Denver, Colorado. I was the eighth child of nine, and my experience was quite different from those of my older siblings. As a child walking down the alley to get to school, I remember feeling special, important, proud, smart, strong, and very different. And I also felt very proud to be Robert Trujillo's daughter. We were the communists on our block. Robert's name would come out in the newspaper, and then we were the communists in the city. However, I often felt the need not to tell my friends who my father was. This secrecy sometimes made me feel afraid and uncomfortable, but it never diminished my pride in him.

I recall vividly when I was a little girl that my Dad slept with a hammer under his bed, because the phone would ring in the middle of the night, and the voice at the other end would threaten my father's life. I felt that he would always protect us.

There was a drug store on the northwest corner of our block, and one time I went into the store to buy a stamp to mail a letter for my older sister, Ruth. She was sending it to her fiancee. The owner said to me, "Is that a communist letter you got, kid?" I got scared because his voice tone was so hateful, and I said, "No it's not!" and I ran home and told my sister. She got quite upset, and called the owner, and she really told him off. She said, "It is none of your business who she was sending the letter to, and furthermore you have no business harassing a child. We will never go into your store again!"

At that time a story on why my father had become a member of the Communist Party came out in the *Denver Post*. The following morning red paint was thrown all over our front porch. Another time, our front-room window was broken with bricks in the middle of the night. Dad had bought a black van, and he woke one morning to find all the windows broken. The FBI agents would park their car across the street from our house and just sit there for hours, keeping surveillance over our house. It wasn't an easy life, and later in life, I seldom let my children sleep at their grandparents' house. But it was our life, and we were taught that we were not victims; we were to tell the truth about all the injustices and never lie. I often got beaten up by two of my siblings for telling the truth, once for telling my father that my brother, Pete, had big parties at our home when my parents were away on a trip. But I didn't care, because I was telling the truth!

My father told us that the belief in Santa Claus was a lie, and since we were poor, he couldn't afford to buy nine kids gifts, especially toys. So after Christmas vacation, all the kids in our third-grade class at Smedley Elementary School were asked by our teacher to stand in front of the class and tell everyone what we got from Santa. Kids got up one by one and told us their long lists of gifts from Santa. But when my turn came, I stood very proud and said, "I got a new pair of jeans and a flannel shirt." Some of the kids giggled, but I had told the truth and didn't care if they laughed at me. Many years later, when I was married and had three children, my dad brought Jarvis Tyner, a communist running for Vice President, along with Gus Hall running for President on the Communist Party ticket, to visit my husband and me at our home. When I shared this story of Santa with Jarvis, he said, "Oh how sad that you never got to believe in Santa. Even us kids who grew up in Harlem believed in him." For some communists, Santa was not a capitalist conspiracy!

I somehow always felt good about not being lied to about Santa Claus. That feeling of being special for knowing the truth has remained with me throughout my life. It has shaped my values and helped me to not fear speaking out and defending what I see as hidden agendas. Being honest has been my guide. My mother reinforced this theme by always saying, "The truth always comes out, so don't lie my hija" (honey).

In addition to the continual harassment Robert and our family endured, there were painful personal events etched in the memory of us kids. For example, I was four years old when Mom had a legal abortion because she had already had three miscarriages, and the doctors at Denver General Hospital advised her to abort. She was in poor health, and the doctors warned that she and the baby were in grave danger. They told her that if she did not have the abortion, she or the baby might die. Dad signed for the abortion, and the guilt almost destroyed Mom's mind. She was depressed and spent a great deal of my childhood in bed. As a child, I vowed to myself that I would die standing rather than to be in bed as she was. I recall my mom holding me close to her breast, and I could feel her anxiety. I felt terrible, and when I was away from her, that feeling stayed with me.

After the abortion, she became pregnant again with my baby brother. Once again the doctors told her that she and the baby were in great danger, and they recommended another abortion. She would not consent. Being a devout Catholic, she felt it was a sin the first time and she could not go through the trauma again. During the nine months that she carried my brother, she had to have a shot every day. She would take me every day on the trolley to Denver General Hospital to get the injection to save her baby.

My brother Richard was born healthy. At first I was jealous of him. Before the birth, my father had sat me on his lap and said, "Hija (endearment for daughter) you are not going to be the baby anymore. Your mother is going to have a new baby." I was four-and-a-half-years old. I had been the baby for those four-and-a-half years. How dare he tell me I was no longer to be the baby! I got over being upset after I got acquainted with the little beautiful bundle of joy. He had the longest eyelashes I had ever seen, and he walked at nine months because there were eight of us children and one of us was always walking him.

There was one step on our staircase that had been patched up with another type of linoleum. One day when my brother Richard (Dickie) was three years old, he was walking up the stairs, and when he got to that strange-looking piece, he would not step on that stair. When I asked him why he wouldn't, he said, "I can't. That's a communist stair!" At that early age he knew the Trujillos were different.

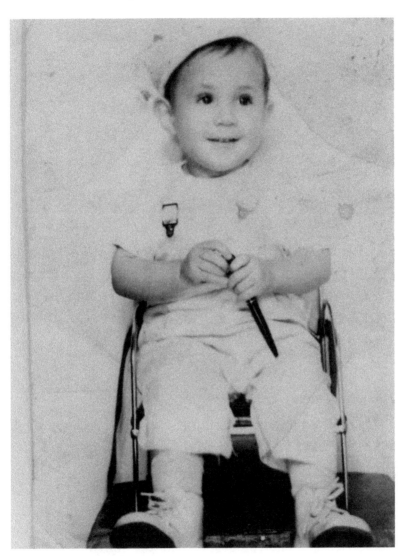

Richard (Baby)

There were also many exciting times during the time of repression for the Communist Party. I recall the wonderful excitement I felt in being close to such an important and serious political organization.

Orlanda and Mary Lou when Richard was born.

Communist Party

I was exposed to political culture in a positive way through the Communist Party. There was a lot of spirit and sincerity and celebration, and I loved it.

The Party's Parties

A world-famous singer and actor, Paul Robeson, sang in our home. I felt special. At times I even felt superior. After all, didn't children of dignitaries feel special? **My** father was a leader, a leader of the truth, of justice, of the poor, of peace, and of love. And **I** was a part of all that goodness. This philosophy gave me a very positive "I'm **okay**" self image. The parties were great. People were all around, happy in their commitment. But the parties had a serious element to them too. We gathered to bring about change, to celebrate in unity for the cause, for the common good.

Robert, his mother Marina and Richard.

Pam Hall was a big hall in west Denver where hundreds of people gathered to celebrate the movement, to increase its growth, to maintain the spirit, and to educate people about socialism. The Communist Party had big parties there with dancing, entertainment, and plenty of food.

One time there were people wall to wall in our eight-room home. There were buckets of pop on ice, and all of us kids went upstairs to the big bathroom and poured dozens of cans of pop into the bathtub, to see all the pop mixed together, all the rainbow colors. As I write this, it occurs to me that maybe like the Communist Party, we children created unity of the different rainbow colors with all the different colors of pop, or maybe we were just being mischievous kids.

One party was at some rich person's house; at least compared to us, the family seemed rich. It was 1948 and my sisters and I sang for a large group of people. Referring to the campaign of Henry A. Wallace, the nominee of the newly formed Progressive Party and a peace candidate, not a communist, we sang, "Wallace is our leader/we shall not be moved/ Wallace is our leader/we shall not be moved/just like the tree that's standing by the water, we shall not be moved." I was six years old, Rena was eight, and Orlanda was ten at that time.

At the parks on Sundays we had huge potluck parties, with the same idea, the same philosophy, talking with people trying to educate them to understand socialism and communism and to join the struggle.

Robert wasn't the only target for harassment. Robert's being a communist hurt all of us kids in different ways. Some of my siblings were harassed at school when my father's name would come out in the newspaper. My sister Orlanda, also called Rosaliene, shared one traumatic experience:

> I was ten years old, and I was attending Smedley Elementary School. Daddy was running for a political office on the Communist Party ticket. [He received 300 votes]. This was now the McCarthy Era, and communists were not too popular. The ridicule by children and teachers for my Daddy's activism was for me, at times, extremely painful. One episode stands out. I was on the playground trying to interact with the other kids when one of them began taunting me with a phrase that still brings tears to my eyes remembering. It was this, "Whistle while you work, Stalin is a jerk. Rosaliene-ee pulled his weenie. Now he does his work." It wasn't long before the other

1948

In 1948 Robert Trujillo applauded during a Denver rally protesting "persecution of communists." Denver Post files.

children joined in. The shame and emotional pain that this awkward, insecure ten-year-old felt at that moment still burns a hole in my soul and is completely indescribable. After that I hated school and my name Rosaliene. I didn't hate the kids because I so desperately wanted to be accepted. What I did to survive all the pain after that was to cover up and deny that I had been so hurt by the kids, and oftentimes I denied that Robert Trujillo was my father.

In another incident during the McCarthy Period in the 1950s, my brother Pete was in the United States Air Force, and the FBI had him discharged, claiming that he was a threat to the Air Force because he was "guilty by association with a Communist." He received an honorable discharge, but the intimidation was terrible. For example, the government officials made it very clear to him that he would never get another government job. The experience put my brother and his family through some painful experiences.

1949

Robert in a paddy wagon arrested in Denver which picketed in October 1949, were from left: Alfonso Sena, Paul Kleinbord, and Robert Trujillo. Denver Post files 1949.

In 1991, at the mural celebration honoring Dad's picture on the Denver Convention Center, my brother Pete spoke of his experience during the McCarthy period.

> About forty years ago, I do not know if it was fortunate or unfortunate that I was in the Air Force during the McCarthy period. McCarthy, the Senator from Wisconsin, believed that, if others were guilty by association, [then I must be.] I had no less then twelve letters of recommendation in my [Air Force] file from everyone who I had worked with, which helped me when I was kicked out of the Air Force.
> I wish I had brought a poem written about four years ago entitled "Pete." The poem started something like this: "my father's great grandfather was a friend of the King of Spain. If this is true, so must I be a friend of the King of Spain." In 1952, when McCarthy was very strong in his "guilty by association" campaign at hearings in Amarillo, Texas, they said that, when I was nine years old, I was at a

[Communist Party] meeting at the YMCA in Denver. They then asked me if that was true, and I said, "I don't remember, but if you say so, then it must be true." They asked me. "Does your father believe in God?" I told them that my father had gone to the eighth grade and he spoke perfect English, why don't you ask him? They said, "your father is a Communist! Then you must be one!" They wanted to give me a dishonorable discharge.

Six months before the three-day campaign to kick me out of the Air Force, the commanding officer of the hospital [I worked in] had given me a letter of recommendation stating that my work performance had gone above and beyond the call of duty and so forth. After the three days of hearings I got an honorable discharge. The crowd broke out cheering and applauding my brother.

Pete, 4 years old.

I recall around the time that my father was expelled from the Party, there was a dishonest informer in Colorado. Many people, including party members experienced the difficulties of the witch-hunt period, and the Party's lack of full-time public national leadership may have been a factor in why my father was expelled from the Party.

I remember a man whom we knew of as Bill Duran (using a fictitious name) joined the party and we were very close to him and his family. In fact, Mom and I babysat for his kids many times. Anyway, he turned out to be an FBI agent and told a lot of lies about members of the Party. So I really don't know exactly why Dad was expelled, although he was a born critic and maybe he was too outspoken in his own opinions, but he didn't seem to hold any bad feelings towards the Party when he was expelled. After the anti-communist hysteria of post-war America faded, Dad was asked to return to the Party, and he gladly did.

From the early 1950's Robert worked on construction and learned about the cement business from his boss. When his boss left, Robert took over the business and went into business for himself as a cement contractor. He called himself a little capitalist. I think he was judging himself, or he may have been joking. As I mentioned, he was a critic and was also self-critical. He did this work for the next seven years. And in his spare time, he worked on various issues of social justice. Even though he was not a Party member during this period, he remained committed to working to educate people towards socialism and communism.

Wearing Glasses

1953

I was eleven years old and was staying with my sister, Ruth, in Colorado Springs, Colorado. I was in her kitchen in the morning when the news came over the radio announcing Ethel and Julius Rosenberg's execution in the electric chair. They had been convicted of being spies for the Soviet Union. My legs turned weak, and I felt I would faint. My father, Robert, was a Communist! This meant that the government could kill my father. Shortly after this, I started wearing glasses. I actually needed glasses, but I'm sure it was reality that I didn't want to see.

Ethel and Julius Rosenberg were executed on June 19, 1953, at Sing Sing Prison, in Ossining, New York. Their execution provoked millions of people throughout the world to demonstrate and protest. Dad said that their execution was used by the government and elites to spread the Cold War anti-Communist hysteria.

In July 1950, Julius Rosenberg had been arrested for "having conspired to commit espionage." By August, Ethel, his wife, and Morton Sobell were arrested. All three of them were charged with being instrumental in conveying the "secret" of the atomic bomb to the Soviet Union. The Rosenbergs were sentenced to death, and Sobell was sentenced to thirty years in prison. Sobell served nineteen years. President Truman was flooded with demands for clemency, but he didn't commute their sentences and neither did his successor, President Eisenhower.

Robert said, "The Rosenbergs were innocent and used as scapegoats to instill fear into not only progressive thinkers, but also those already involved in the struggle. This was also a tactic to discourage people from joining the Communist Party." Robert asserted that this tactic of fear was McCarthy's goal.

The leaders, organizers, and workers of the Communist Party give a different account of this period in America's history. Robert said that, given the effects of the Depression, Roosevelt's New Deal saved the country from collapse and from a revolution. The reason the Red scare intensified was because the Communist Party influences were very strong at this time because the masses were out of work, desperate, and ready for answers, and the government was really worried about how the people were being influenced by the Communist Party's program. The Party's program was offering the workers information about the root causes of the Depression and, foremost, alternatives to their problems. The U.S. government needed to give the people some

concrete solutions before the masses turned to revolution. So the New Deal was created to prevent a
workers' revolution.

Robert added that none of the advances that came out of
the New Deal were given to the American people out of the
kindness of the government. It was the Communist and other
leftist origanization that spearheaded these advances. These
leftist groups were becoming very effective in pushing for and
demanding measures such as worker's compensation, social
security, and welfare, as well as many other benefits that
helped the unemployed. These measures were put in place to
help the U.S. economic system recover.

Although the Communist Party was a revolutionary party
working towards changing the system, basic survival was its
major focus during the Depression

Marx stated that in order to achieve a just society, the masses
had to organize and bring it forward. So it was crucial for the
American government to create the New Deal so as to put the
brakes on the people's struggle towards this end.

American trade unionist William Z. Foster wrote:

> To sum-up the New Deal…it was a greatly increased
> centralization of the Federal government and its
> intensified intervention in economic life along the
> following main lines: (a) pouring of government
> billions into the banks, railroads, etc. to save them
> from threatening bankruptcy; (b) raising of the price
> level through inflation (devaluation of the dollar,
> immense bond issues, etc.), code-price-fixing and
> organized restriction of agricultural and industrial
> production; (c) liquefying of billions of dollars of
> the banks that were frozen in unpayable mortgages
> on farms and homes by extension of payment peri-
> ods on these mortgages; (d) "priming the industrial
> pump" and easing the workers' unrest by large
> government capital investment in public works; (e)
> tinkering up by law the worst breaks in the capital-
> ist banking and credit system, including supervision

of the stock exchange, sale of foreign bonds, etc.; (f) intensified struggle for world markets—bigger navy, air fleet, army, new tariff agreements, etc.; (g) throwing a bone to the starving masses of unemployed and aged by allotting them niggardly Federal relief and skeleton pensions; (h) granting of rights of the workers to organize into labor unions; (I) organized subsidies to farmers for reducing production. [10]

In short, the New Deal was calculated to help the capitalist system survive and thrive by deflecting the pressure that was being directed towards the U.S. government.

The next decade, the 1950s, saw the beginning of the Civil Rights movement and the unrest and rebellion it sparked in the United States and around the world. This period of turbulence ignited Robert's spirit of passion, because it gave him the opportunity and audience to continue to spread his belief in socialism.

---

[10] "The New Deal," American Trade Unionism by William Z. Foster, (International Publishers, 1947.)

Chapter *4*

Times of Turbulence (1960–1980)

As the Civil Rights Movement took hold in the early1960's, the country sat poised to usher in two decades of civil disorder, rebellion, and a variety of crises, which spawned additional Civil Rights movements.

Robert characteristically was in the heat of it all in Colorado as he continued to practice and educate people about socialism and communism. He connected the injustices, institutional racism, individual hatreds and acts of violence, and wars and discrimination to the American system. He explained that these are all rooted in America's social and economic structure.

In an interview in <u>The Denver Post</u> in 1967, reporter Leonard Larsen asked Robert about the war in Vietnam:

> "Your main concern then is with the war in Vietnam, over and above any other problem of the country?" "Yes, that's right," replied Robert. 'These riots that are happening all over the country come as a result of the failures of our government to take care of the problems of our country. They are too busy spending enormous wealth, besides [taking] the lives of our boys, to carry out this crazy war in Vietnam for the sake of profiteers who want to get richer and richer every day. Congress is demanding that LBJ cut down on the domestic problems. What do they mean by the domestic problems? They mean the poor people.

Don't give the poor people anything. Just draft them into the Army. They've got the people believing our boys have to fight and die in Vietnam to stop the danger of the Communists coming over here and taking over our country. Isn't that the domino theory?—If Vietnam falls, Southeast Asia falls; the Philippines, the Hawaiian Islands, California, everything else falls. This is what they preach every day on the radio and television and in the newspapers. They say we are in Vietnam to stop Communism. That's the biggest lie they could tell.[11]

The peace movement was a direct result of this war that was killing not only millions of Vietnamese, but also thousands of American soldiers. Robert helped organized peace rallies in Colorado at Rocky Flats, and the State Capitol, and in surrounding areas.

During the Vietnam War in 1971, I wrote the following poem about my father:

My Dad

It took me years to see the light, to understand, to lose the fright. A lot of people used to say: he's confused in a funny way.

I was very young at heart and did not want to face that part. Society says of him that he's wrong and always has been. He believes in Christianity, but more than that, in humanity!

So he is different from all the rest. Yet, wrong or right, he's done his best to help the man who is poor, the races that suffer to the core. His greatest ambition is to stop the war.

He's gone to jail for what he believes. Trying to explain, like Christ, he bleeds.

---

[11]   Leonard Larson, "Denver Communist Struggles On," *The Denver Post*, October 15, 1967.

He is a Communist! He is my dad. A lot of times it has been sad,
but all the time I've been glad that this great man is my dad.

He'll not go down in history: he's a simple man, a lot like me.
Robert Trujillo is his name. Most people judge and blame.

Hear what he has to say, and maybe you'll understand his way.

My youngest brother, Richard, recalls:

During 9 and 10 grade, kids taunted me a lot about my
father being a communist. But this one much older guy who
was eighteen took it out on me as if I was a communist and
every time I would run into him, he would punch me like
a man. I was scared to death of him. But then one day it all
ended as abruptly as it started. I guess I just wasn't afraid of
him any more, and he must have sensed that.

I started to become religiously and politically aware at the
age of thirteen. My dad let a lot of Communist Party members and sympathizers sleep at our home when they came into
town for meetings, seminars, recruitment, and rallies. I had
the honor of meeting Gus Hall, Henry Winston, and Angela
Davis, who were top leaders of the Communist Party. I also
had the privilege of meeting Dr. Martin Luther King Jr., Cesar
Chavez, and Jesse Jackson, who were not communists but
were great activists.

My father was in the movement for equal rights, civil rights,
jobs, justice, socialism and communism. I joined him, and I
attended anti-Vietnam War demonstrations, and I was part of
the United Farm Workers struggle.

There was also a group started in Denver, Colorado by
Corky Gonzales, who created the activist Chicano group the
"Crusade For Justice." One of the actions the Crusade was
associated with was the United Farm Workers' boycott against
the growers of iceberg lettuce. The United Farm Workers were
demanding better wages and living conditions. During the
start of the Chicano movement, the "Chicano Teatro" was
born, and many young Chicano actors were touring the country with theater acts aimed at educating their audiences about
the political injustices of the times, including those of the farm
workers.

There were other issues we were struggling for, like the struggle to keep drugs out of our neighborhoods. Dad and I used to go to meetings called Fishermen's meetings at the Crusade for Justice every Wednesday night, discussing what issues we should focus our attention on.

A nationwide recession that began in 1959 was still going on in 1963. Over one-and-a half-million Blacks were unemployed due to the recession, and of course racism was a major factor: the Black unemployment rate was twice that of whites.

During the Civil Rights period, on August 28,1963, when I was sixteen-years-old, I went to the "March on Washington" with my dad where Martin Luther King Jr. made his famous "I Have A Dream" speech. The march took place to demand jobs and freedom. More than 250,000 attended it. My dad and I went on a bus with fifty-eight people. We had people playing guitars and singing folksongs and revolutionary songs. We all joined in singing along with them. We traveled by day and slept in churches at night in Hannibal, Missouri, Indianapolis, Indiana, and a town in West Virginia, and we were treated to wonderful potlucks and theater for those three nights.

The morning of the fourth day we arrived in Washington D.C. As we were going into the city on the interstate highway, both sides of the highway were jammed with buses leading in and out of the city. Trainloads of people had come from the northeast, from New York, New Jersey, and Pennsylvania, and from Illinois. This was more people than had ever taken part in a civil-rights demonstration in this country. It also had extensive television coverage. The amount of humanity and energy was unbelievable! We filled the entire park in front of the Lincoln Memorial and the Washington Monument.

Then, when I was seventeen-years-old, and again when I was eighteen my father took me to New York City. Each time, we spent about five days there. He took me to the Communist Party conventions, which were very educational for me. There was a great deal of camaraderie and parties.

I was a teenager when the war in Vietnam started. When I came of age, my father did everything he could to keep me out of the Vietnam War, including sending me to college and paying all of my expenses. When I was in college, I had a student deferment. I dropped out of college in 1968 to get married, and I went to work to support my family. I was immediately reclassified 1A and ordered to take my physical for induction into the Army. I filled out the form as a Conscientious Objector, and that was turned down. I thought about going to Canada to avoid the draft in order to avoid killing or being killed. The war ended, so that was a great relief for my family and me. I lost a lot of friends in that war, for nothing. There was nothing worthwhile about that insane war.

The Vietnam War was very unpopular all around the country. On college campuses, anti-war demonstrations were taking place. For example, one of the largest and most disruptive protests against the war in Vietnam was at Kent State University in Ohio. The National Guard killed four students! This incident brought out hundreds of thousands of people demonstrating in the streets. The National Guard at Kent State looked like Nazi storm troopers as they moved through the demonstrators using tear gas and clubbing students with their nightsticks. It was absolutely horrible!

As a result of the four students being assassinated, more violent demonstrations began to happen around the country. In 1968 the S.D.S., "Students for a Democratic Society," a college-born, grass-roots organization, and a lot of different progressive groups disrupted the Democratic National Convention, trying to speak on the floor during the convention in Chicago. They were protesting the war in Vietnam and other issues such as poverty and racism, and they were also protesting against the nominating process. There was a lot of violence surrounding the anti-war protests during the Vietnam War, and the police and the National Guard instigated much of it.

About the same time, during the civil-rights period, many people were killed and brutalized during demonstrations. On national television, for example, there were scenes of Black people being brutalized, hit with billy clubs, electronic stun guns, hosed with water, and tear gassed, and setting large dogs loose on the crowds was common practice.

During this period President John F. Kennedy was assassinated in 1963, Civil Rights leader Dr. Martin Luther King Jr.

was assassinated in 1968, a front-running presidential candidate, Senator Robert Kennedy, was assassinated in 1968, and three civil-rights workers were killed in Mississippi.

In 1968 my father also went to the "Poor People's Campaign" in Washington. The main purpose of the Poor People's Campaign was jobs, income, and housing.

One person that the media claimed was accidentally killed during the riots in 1970 was Ruben Salazar, a journalist who often wrote about Chicanos for the Los Angeles Times. My nephew, Frankie, was at this demonstration, and I recall him telling me about this incident, claiming that a police bullet killed Ruben Salazar.

My experiences included handing out the Communist Party paper, "The Daily World." I also met some famous people such as labor leaders, poets, artists, musicians, lawyers, and Chicano actors. I met Cesar Chavez, the leader of the United Farm Workers, Mexican poet Albelardo (Lalo) Delgado, actors Jane Fonda and her brother Peter Fonda and the Hallinan Brothers, criminal-defense lawyers who defended Communist Party members.

Mary Lou said, like Richard's, my life was shaped by my father's politics during the 1960's and 70's. My political fever started to sizzle. Because I was raised by a communist father-and by this time my mother had also joined the Communist Party-politics were as much a part of our family as Catholicism is to most Mexicans. By this time my parents had been twice to the Soviet Union and once to Cuba and got a first hand account of Socialism. I got involved with my parents in the protests against the war in Vietnam, in The United Farm Workers struggle, and the boycotts against Coors, as well as other civil-rights issues like equal education for all ethnic groups efforts to and end discriminatory educational practices in the schools such as tracking students. "Tracking" is the process of placing students in groups or classes based on skills and abilities in Language Arts and Mathematics. This process, while intended to be fair, at times was used to discriminate and place students in groups that were below their potential. For the most part, teachers and educators value the best interests of the students, but I personally sat in on meetings where this was not always the case.

In 1978 I organized a large group against police brutality after my husband and I had watched the police clubbing young people across the street from our home. There was a demonstration at Columbus Park, at 38th and Navajo, to demand that the name of the park be changed to La Raza Park. The police were called in to break up the demonstration, and they chased the crowd all the way up to 38th and Tejon, where we lived. I was appalled! We named ourselves "The People's Coalition Against Police Brutality." I worked for quite some time as the chair and spokesperson for the coalition. We were getting some opposition, and my father told me not to get discouraged. He said, "Hija always remember with organizing: when there's a lot of opposition to what you are doing, you must be doing something right!" We were very effective raising some important concerns and effecting some changes, like helping create a committee to ensure that brutalities by police would not occur. Yet the reality of police brutality is still a problem in Denver and around the country.

My children were little, and at times I had them with me at demonstrations. My husband was always working, and, for the most part, he did not mind my interest in the struggle, but he did not fully comprehend what we were all about. His family was Republican, and, as you can imagine, we had very different political views. My husband finally realized he couldn't stop me. We had several conflicts over my activism, and because he was raised to believe in all the "machismo," we disagreed on gender issues. My husband felt a woman's place was in the home, but my father felt I was to become another Angela Davis. I had to find out who I was.

The demonstrations stimulated my passion, affecting me to fill empowered and having a voice in our society.

The civil-rights demonstrators around the country made some gains. President Lyndon B. Johnson took office following the assassination of John F. Kennedy. Johnson completed Kennedy's term and then was re-elected. His most important accomplishments were the Civil Rights Act of 1964-inspired by King's "I Have a Dream" speech of the preceding summer-and the Voting Rights Act of 1965. With popular support, President Johnson was responsible for designing additional

"Great Society" legislation, including Medicare, Medicaid, the Public Broadcasting System, the Environmental Protection Agency, and the Aid to Education Act, along with the War on Poverty.

The Aid to Education Act allowed many of us minorities to enroll in higher education. I started my university career after 11 years of marriage and three children. In 1975 I received my Bachelor of Arts (with Distinction) in Political Science at the University of Colorado. As I continued my education in 1982 I received my Master of Arts in Political Science at the University of Colorado. Then, in 1994, I received a Doctor of Philosophy in Education-Social Multicultural and Bilingual Foundation, Policy and Practice at the University of Colorado at Boulder.

I had attended a Marxist School in California in 1973, taking my thirteen-year-old daughter with me. The adults were impressed at how easily she grasped the basic concepts of Marxist theory. I met Angela Davis during the last class. She just walked in and introduced herself and talked with the students. Angela Davis had had a profound effect on me even before I met her. I admired her strength and dignity in standing up for people who were incarcerated for their political involvement. She went to prison for her leadership in defending justice for all people.

I traveled to Cuba in 1978, wanting to add the raw data of experience to my masters' thesis (1982) which examined and compared the educational systems of the United States and Cuba. I visited schools and met with university professors, students, and ordinary Cuban people, and learned a great deal from them. I attended the International Youth Festival in Havana with forty thousand youth from all over the world. I finally got to see and hear Fidel Castro speak at a mass rally after waiting six hours. In the middle of reading his speech, he found a mistake he had made and paused to say, "Every time we make a mistake, we must correct it on the spot so that we will remember not to make that same mistake again."

That was a peak experience for me. When I remember the small, beautiful island under socialism and the beauty of the Cuban culture, especially the carino (affection) of the Cuban people. It still awakens excitement in me. For instance, I was on a bus coming back from a ride around the countryside and I must have looked a sight, with my long curly hair all over in the humid climate. A Cuban guy from way on the other side of the bus motioned to me non-verbally, asking if I wanted a shot of tequila. I nodded yes. So he poured me a drink and passed it to me in a tin cup by way of about ten passengers.

At times I didn't know if it was the Cuban culture I was seeing or if it was the socialist system. I'm sure it was a combination of both. The Cubans are a very loving people, and my experience there left me with a strong positive impression of the people, their culture, their island, and their socialist government. Another time, I was walking up a narrow street and a woman handed me a thin loaf of fresh, warm bread and gave me a beautiful smile. I thanked her in Spanish, and I remember thinking, "No wonder the rich man wanted to keep Cuba; it was a haven for the rich."

As I walked through the Museum of the Revolution, I was moved to tears as I saw pictures of pre-Revolutionary Cuba, of starvation, ignorance, poverty, suffering and pain. I compared what I saw in the streets of Havana with the children playing on beaches, and imagined what it was like before the revolution, when the beaches were restricted to the rich. A nine-year-old child was asking me intelligent political questions about world peace: "Are you in favor of the neutron bomb, and are you for world peace?"

As I was viewing the atrocities that the people had lived with during the Batista Regime, I saw a poster on the wall of the museum that read, "Cada soldado caido, es una raiz" ("Every fallen soldier is a root"), and I broke down crying thinking of my beautiful twenty-three-year-old nephew, Frankie, who had recently been murdered.

In my diary in 1978 I wrote about Cuba: "There are still elements of the class society. There is a difference in people. The more educated seem more secure and confident. And the ones who look poor are kind of mistrusting or maybe curious. I don't know; Mary Lou, look who's mistrusting? Really, I find myself wanting so to believe in the trust and brotherhood I am told is all around me. And yet, when someone pays my way on a bus or when the cab driver wouldn't take the dollar for my cab fee, I ask myself, 'Are they doing this to impress the tourist?' When I have never seen anyone doing these things, I tend to question their motives. Yeah, woman, remember: I was raised in the U.S.!"

I remember that when Dad was interviewed by news staff writer Eric Lawlor in January 21, 1979 and asked whether any of his children were in the [Communist] Party, he said, "No, but I haven't raised bourgeoisie either. In fact one daughter went to Havana [Cuba] last year for the International Youth Festival. The experience delighted her. She told me when she got back that the children in Cuba are better educated [politically] than many adults here in the United States."[12]

Another area in which Party members were involved during this period was the industrial unions. The Communist Party has had an active role in the labor movement in the United States. The party took a major hand in founding the first industrial unions in the United States. For decades the members of the Party have contributed their support for the unions.

Dad went often to Pueblo, Colorado, a steel-mill town 150 miles south of Denver. He joined with other Party members who had formed a Party club that organized and held public meetings against the job discrimination that was going on at the Colorado Fuel and Iron Company. They were protesting CF&I's practice of stratifying jobs according to ethnicity, whereby White workers got the highest paid jobs, the Mexican Americans worked the manual-labor jobs, and African Americans worked the coke ovens and the company owned-railway.

The climate in the 1960's and 70's was one of change, excitement, and hope as we participated in the democratic process.

As time passed, my father remained committed to his pursuit of justice. Whenever he saw an injustice, he joined in to fight against it. In 1969 he got involved with a group that was later called "The Denver 14." They came together to defend the rights of Colorado farm workers before the Colorado Legislature.

---

[12]   Eric Lawlor, "State Communist Still Battling Bourgeoisie," "The Rocky Mountain News", January 21, 1979.

Chapter *5*

"The Denver 14," May 6, 1969

"Blessed are they who hunger and thirst for justice, for they shall be satisfied," (Matthew 5:6)

Prelude to "The Denver 14"

Dad continued to thirst for justice. Along with thirteen others he was arrested for defending Colorado farm workers. Leading up to their arrest, several bills were introduced in the State General Assembly to give farm workers some collective bargaining rights. The bills were rejected in the State House of Representatives.

In 1969, Rep. Ben Klein, D-Denver, introduced two bills on the subject of the farm workers. House Bill 1032 would put farm employers who have five or more employees working more than six months of each year under Workers' Compensation. It provided medical, dental, unemployment, death, and injury benefits to workers out of a state fund supported by employer contributions. The employers would also benefit by such coverage because it would reduce liability-insurance premiums and provide needed resources to take care of employees injured on the job, thus reducing employers' out- of-pocket expenditures.

The House Labor and Employment Relations Committee approved this measure. Yet more still needed to be done. Rep. Robert Schaeffer, R-Boyero, went to bat for this farm reform. An effective legislative piece was needed immediately in order to put substantial numbers of Colorado farm laborers under the provisions of the Colorado Labor Peace Act.

Ben Klein's second proposed bill, House Bill 1033, made a farm operator with eight or more employees subject to the provisions of the Colorado Labor Peace Act. The Peace Act provided ways for employees to seek outside support in getting a union and bargaining rights from an employer. Small farmers, along with the large farm operators, feared the bill because they argued: "We get low prices, so we can't pay farm labor a higher wage." An attempt was made to rewrite H.B. 1033 with the hope that it could be made agreeable to most people involved.

To draw attention to the plight of Colorado farm workers, and in support of these in farm-labor laws that were being considered by the Colorado General Assembly, nine members of the "Denver Witnesses for Human Dignity" participated in a nine-day fast. Despite this effort, the bill was killed. In fact all the bills introduced by Rep. Ben Klein on behalf of improving conditions for the farm workers were defeated. To attract attention and reinvent support, the "Denver Witnesses for Human Dignity" deposited coffins in the Capitol. Twenty-six demonstrators carried six imitation coffins into the State Capitol and deposited them there. The coffins symbolized the dead bills that would have supported the farm workers. In 1969, *the Denver Post* reported that the demonstrators had placed black coffins that bore the white lettering: "Mr. Education," "Consumer Protection," "Mr. and Mrs. Housing," "Police Respect, Law and Order," "Mrs. Welfare," and "Miss Farm Labor." Members of the group carried signs saying "Justice is Dead," "We Lament the Death of Justice," "The Law Must Respect People," "Viva La Causa" and "Justice Is Dead in Colorado." ["Coffins' Deposited in Capitol." *the Denver Post* 6 May 1969.]

The "coffin" demonstration led the way for an even more aggressive, though nonviolent. demonstration on May 6. 1969. These demonstrators became known as "The Denver 14". Among them was Robert Trujillo. This group came together because of their concern for the plight of the farm workers. My father did not know any of the members. None of them were affiliated with the Communist Party, and they came from all walks of life.

The Denver 14, May 6, 1969

I recall the excitement in our family when we heard that 'The Denver 14" had been arrested, especially because our father was one of them. The smell of fresh beans, green pork chile, and homemade tortillas filled the rooms of our home in north Denver. Some of my brothers and sisters and their children were at my parents' house in north Denver at the time the story came out on the evening news. We all sat taking in all the details as their arrest was shown on TV. I remember feeling so proud of my father because he had the courage to take such a risk that I ran over and hugged Mom. My older sister Orlanda was in the hospital having surgery at the time of their arrest. We were all concerned about her, yet inspired by the stance of the Denver 14.

These are the events surrounding "The Denver 14" and a letter from The Denver 14 Defense Committee. On Wednesday May 6, 1969, fourteen demonstrators forced their way into the Colorado Senate Chambers. They were protesting the legislature's failure to pass twenty-two bills dealing with farm labor, consumer protection, welfare, housing, education, and law enforcement-all bills that would have helped Colorado's working class and Colorado's poor.

The demonstrators entered a side door of the Senate. One of the demonstrators knocked on the door, and Senator Wayne Denny, R Cortez, thinking another member of the Senate wanted in, opened it. Members of the group seized the door and swung it open. They shoved Wayne Denny aside and went directly to the rostrum.

One presiding officer, Lieutenant Governor Mark Hogan, tried to persuade the group to leave and take its protest elsewhere so the Senate could begin its business. The demonstrators refused. The protest group consisted of five women and nine men, who including two priests, a nun, and a minister, as well as my father, the chairman of the Colorado Communist Party.

Five Democratic senators remained in their seats—George Brown and Roger Cisneros of Denver, J.D. MacFarlane of Pueblo, Anthony Vollack of Arvada, and Kirt Wagner of Las Animas—while the rest of the senators fled the chamber. Lieutenant Gov. Mark Hogan told the demonstrators he felt they were using the wrong method of expressing their protest. Nonetheless, the demonstrators refused to leave the chamber, and a spokesman for the group said they would not leave "until you pass these bills."

When the police arrived, they had to carry thirteen of the protesters out of the chambers. The fourteenth protester walked out. All were arrested, handcuffed, and taken to the city jail. "The Denver 14" spent one day and one night in jail. Some family members of the protestors put up their homes to bail them out. I was instructed beforehand by my father to put up his home to bail him and several of the protesters out of jail.

One of "The Denver 14," Catholic priest Craig Hart, said there was a lot of energy among the demonstrators and that it was an incredible learning experience for him. He added they passed special legislation afterwards to insure that this kind of incident didn't happen again. Dad said it was emotional and exciting being involved and going to jail with the fourteen dedicated people.

On January 24, 1970, 13 of "The Denver 14" were acquitted of the charges of illegal assembly and of obstructing the State Senate in May of 1969. Recuperating from an automobile accident, Mrs. Sheila Ivers was not at the trial. Her trial began on February 2, 1970.[13]

Mom, my sister Orlanda, my brother Richard, and I were at the trial when the verdicts were announced. We were thrilled when the judge read the verdicts. People were hugging and shouting with joy and relief. It was wonderful to witness justice being done. In the evening we all attended a huge celebration Victory Party at someone's home in east Denver for "The Denver 14". I recall that there was a boycott against Coors Beer at the time due to discrimination allegations against Coors.

---

[13]   [See articles on "The Denver 14 " in Appendix, p. 179.]

Someone brought some Coors beer, and someone else poured the beer down the drain!

Who's to know whether the demonstrators felt they would influence the legislators to reverse their decisions about killing all the bills supporting the farm workers. But they definitely exposed the lack of sensitivity and the injustice of the decision of the legislators. "The Denver 14" made their protest a first in the history of Colorado, and they also made it known loudly and clearly that the farm workers' needs had been discounted, disrespected, and ignored.

Effects of the Denver 14

An important question for future research is whether the action of "The Denver 14" affected the legislators, at a later time, to pass any legislation to improve the living and working conditions for the farm workers.

In a conversation on March 15, 2000, Craig Hart (a former Catholic priest and one of "The Denver 14", said:

> That's a very good question. The legislators did not meet with us, and I don't know if anything happened. The farm workers finally successfully formed a union after several years of a boycott [The United Farm Workers Union], but I am not aware just how that particular incident may have affected improving the working and living conditions of the farm workers here in Colorado or elsewhere. I believe your father would have answered this question you asked with something like this: Because of the capitalist system, problems may go away but they will show up in another place at another time. The system itself works so that systemic [development] doesn't change things, at least not the basic things that benefit the capitalist system. Such is the case with police brutality and racism.

According to personal correspondence with former legislator Ben Klein, on March 27, 2000, "Yes, I introduced the bills for legislation in 1969 for the farm workers. Although the bills were defeated, big farmers have had to take care of improving the housing conditions for the farm workers. So housing conditions for the farm workers have seen substantial improvement." Mr. Klein added that this improvement might have been ten years after the Denver 14 demonstration.

From my perspective, what the Denver 14 accomplished is this: By invading the Colorado Senate Chambers while the legislators were in session, they brought the issue of the farm workers to the public. They had full media coverage, giving them tremendous publicity and exposure. Thus people came to know about injustice and about how unconcerned the legislators were about the terrible conditions of the farm workers. The protest also brought support for the farm workers from people who had not previously known about these things.

For our family, the result of our father's activism was that he was often called a commie, a hippie, and a crazy. But in some respects, he was given way too much credit. For example, some people accused him of being the instigator of The Denver 14, when in fact he was just one of the participants. From this experience I learned the importance of standing up for what you believe in, championing those less fortunate, and not being deterred by what others might say or think of you because you are willing to stand up for a good cause.

How family members experienced our father's beliefs varied and each of their account is unique. You can judge how having a "Red" father affected us in the following chapter on my sibling stories.

Chapter 6

Shifting Voices

The Stories of Robert Trujillo's Children

Between 1927 and 1947 Robert and Edna had nine children. Their names, in order are Frank, Ruth, Fred, Gilbert, Pete, Orlanda, Marina, Mary Lou, and Richard. All of us experienced our father's activism differently. The following are stories of four of my siblings: Frank, Ruth, Marina, and Richard, as well my own and my husband Virgil's.

Frank D. Trujillo was born on September 5, 1927. Excerpts of Frank's story begin in Chapter 2, The Great Depression.

Frank shared with me additional experiences with our Dad and Mom, as well as experiences with discrimination:

> In 1942, Dad and I worked in Colorado Springs at Camp Carson as laborers, helping to build the army base. Dad moved our family from Walsenberg, Colorado, to Colorado Springs, Colorado, in the spring of 1942. In the fall of that year, I went to Colorado Springs High School as a sophomore.
>
> In 1943 we moved to Eaton, Colorado, to work in the beet fields. The first time I encountered racial discrimination was in Eaton. I was sixteen, and I would drive my brothers and sisters from the farm to the city movie theater. They asked us to sit in the back of the theater. When I asked why, the man said that our breath smelled of garlic. Needless to say, we did not sit in the back rows. He called the manager,

but we refused to move. The manager said that if we didn't move, he would call the police, but the police never showed up. Dad told me he was proud of the fact that we stood our ground.

In 1944 we moved again, this time to Denver, Colorado, where my father was given a job managing a co-op grocery store. I managed to graduate from West High School in 1945. I joined the United States Navy shortly after my graduation in Denver, Colorado. On a ten-day leave from San Diego, California, my father, wearing a business suit, my mother, in her best Sunday dress, and I, wearing my Navy dress uniform, went to Fort Collins, Colorado on some deliveries that my father had to make. At lunchtime we went into a restaurant, and we sat down and waited and waited. No one took our order. When we finally asked for service we were told, "We do not serve Mexicans." The same thing happened at the second restaurant. We all got very upset, and my Dad said to us, "What the hell is going on?" We got up and walked out. We didn't raise a ruckus because we knew we'd be thrown in jail. We saw the small sign we hadn't noticed on the window on our way out the door: "We Cater to White Trade Only." We went to a third restaurant, and we were finally served.

I also encountered frequent discrimination when I drove a city bus in Denver, Colorado, from 1953 to 1989. One incident, and there were many, was when I was driving a bus for Denver Tramway. Some people from Mexico who didn't speak English got on my bus and sat behind me. We talked in Spanish the whole trip. Another couple, on their way off the bus, stopped and the man said, "Why in the hell don't you speak in English?" Because of incidents like this, my wife Angelina and I raised four children not to speak Spanish, so that they would not be discriminated against. This is the only regret my wife and I have in our life.

I attended the University of Northern Colorado in Greeley, Colorado, from 1946 until 1949, using my GI Bill. It was then called Colorado State Teachers' College. My experience in college was very positive. My professors and the students treated me as an equal. Professor Wilmington, my Humanities and History professor, was great. And Professor Candelaria, my Spanish teacher, was an excellent role model for me.

Today, I remember my father for his teachings of peace and justice to create harmony. He taught us never to use violence in resolving conflicts, including wars. My father retired from construction work in 1965 because he didn't approve of the War in Vietnam. He didn't want his taxes going to kill American boys and Vietnamese people.

My sister, Ruth, was born in 1928 in Walsenburg, Colorado. Her account is as follows:

I was fourteen years old when the Second World War started. Dad found a job in Colorado Springs, Colorado, where Camp Carson [now named Fort Carson] was being built.

One of my older cousins told me her brother had Alzheimer's. He couldn't remember what happened yesterday, but talked vividly about things that happened years ago. I introduced myself to him at a wedding and I asked him if he remembered my parents. He said, "Of course," and he told me this story about Dad. "We had many children, and we were very poor that year, and Roberto came to visit us. I told him about the fact that I had been to the welfare office in San Luis and they refused to help me. Roberto said he would pick me up the next morning and we'd go back to the welfare office in San Luis. In an hour and a half they gave me help for the winter. Your father was an intelligent man. I was very grateful. Had it not been for him, we would have had a

very bad winter." We both had tears in our eyes. I
thanked him for the story.

Many years after I was married, I asked Dad,
"What did you do with the money we made on the
farm?" "I'll tell you hija," Dad answered. "I put the
money we all made in the bank in Greeley. Then we
came to Denver. We rented a house, and I looked for
a house to buy, and when I found this house, I took
the money out and used it as a down payment on
the house. And when I die, this house will be sold
and it will be divided among our nine children." I
said, "Dad, I really wish you would leave me just a
portion of your mind." He replied, "You must learn
and educate yourself. All you have to do is read,
read, read, and then educate others." I will always
be grateful to Dad, who instilled in us children the
value of education, not only for the boys, but for
us girls also. For example, one morning Mom told
me she did not want me to go to school because she
wanted me to help her wash clothes. Dad noticed
I wasn't getting ready for school, and he asked me
why, and I told him, and he said, "Get ready. Go.
I'll help her." Dad was a salesman for the Raleigh
Product Company at that time, so he chose his own
hours.

This is Marina's (Rena's), account of growing up in our family. She was the seventh child, and I was the eighth. We grew
up together and were very close as teenagers, as we were only
two years apart. Here are Rena's recollections:

I was born in 1940, in Walsenburg, Colorado. My
brothers and sisters used to tease me because I had
a light complexion. They said I was an orphan they
had found in a basket on the doorstep.

Mom told me I was lucky to be alive because
when I was born, the umbilical cord was wrapped
around my neck. I came into this world black from
a lack of oxygen.

As the story goes, Mother was sewing a mattress when she started having labor pains. She told my brother Fred to go to the courthouse and tell Dad. Dad was in jail for having taken part in a political demonstration, parading without a permit. Frank [my oldest brother] ran to find the doctor, who was a notorious drunk. But Frank found him and came back in time for the doctor to deliver me. I was born blue-eyed and blonde-haired. Over the years, my eyes turned hazel in color, and my hair became medium brown. I was four when our family moved to the house on Tejon Street [in Denver]. The house had a back kitchen stairway that was connected to a front stairway that went down into the dining room. My sister Mary Lou and Orlanda and I loved to run up one stairway and down the other. (We probably drove Mom crazy.) We loved to play hide-and-go- seek because it was—or at least seemed—like such a big house. We could hide for hours, and nobody could find us. I remember one time I was hiding in a huge trunk in a big upstairs closet. Orlanda was searching for me, and my heart was beating fast, and I was excited until she found me.

Mom was real good. She never used to yell at us. Dad was more businesslike, usually very preoccupied with his politics and with his work. He frequently would take part in meetings of his fellow communists at home or at Palm Hall on West Colfax in Denver.

When Mary Lou was six and I was eight and Orlanda was ten, Dad would have us get up on the stage at the meeting hall and sing union songs. We didn't know what we were singing, but the adults in the audience loved our performance. I still remember some of the phrases of these songs. "Black and white together, we shall not be moved…" and "There once was a union maid, who never was afraid of company goons…"

Dad was a generous and affectionate man. Often, he made huge buckets of tamales to take to his party meetings, and everybody was welcome to eat as many as they wanted. I might add, our father was a fabulous cook! When he had meetings at home, we kids loved to get our tamales and our pops and go upstairs and shake the bottles of pop and let them squirt all over the bathtub!

Our life at home was lots of fun when we were children. Christmases were especially delightful, even though we never got presents. All we had was a Christmas tree and candy. I remember walking with Dad, who held my hand, along Tejon Street to buy a Christmas tree. Mary Lou and Orlanda would go with us too. The joy of Christmas was just in the sharing and the love we felt.

One of my fondest memories of summertime is of Dad going to buy a huge watermelon, which he always left overnight in a tub of ice. The next evening, we would eat it when he got home around 8 o'clock.

Dad was affectionate, and Mom too. Mom was always in the kitchen cooking. Dad used to say, "Who wants to walk down to the creamery and get a cow cream?" A cow cream was like a swirl like Dairy Cream, only richer. I loved them, especially the chocolate ones.

In the kitchen of our home was a wood-burning stove, and the family liked to sit around in the kitchen, which was warm and cozy even on the coldest days. I remember when Mom's dad, Epitacio Sanchez, came to visit. He was a widower, and he really loved us. He had the brightest blue eyes, which had a sparkle in them. He was a happy man. I was sad when he died in 1947. I was seven.

We used to go to the San Luis Valley three or four times a year to see Grandpa Sanchez and Dad's mother. Grandma Marina's first husband [and the father of Robert] was Francisco Trujillo, who had moved to the Valley from Tierra Amarilla, New Mexico, where he had been born. He died at age 45 of tuberculosis. Her second husband was Patricio Valdez.

My (Mary Lou's) own recollections of my life in a communist Mexican-American family are as follows.

When I was a child, my father went to a meeting in Washington D.C. for three weeks. It seemed like forever until he returned. When he walked in the house, the three of us girls ran into his arms. He was fat, so we all fit in his arms real well. He would have us kids all sit in a circle, and he would tell us all about his experience. I still teach all my classes in a circle.

Another time he went to the Indian Reservation in South Dakota and he brought us kids some musical instruments made by the Native Americans. They were made with real bird feathers. After we felt the joy of our new instruments, his voice became serious, and he shared his experience with us. He said that we should share and never be selfish or take what little we had for granted, because our Native American brothers and sisters had so little to live on.

He then told us the history of the Native Americans and how this land was their land and foreign invaders stole their land by the same inhumane means that they continue to use around the world today. He always stressed the need for true brotherhood among all people. We were socialized to be internationalist rather than nationalist. Dad said segregation was the tool of the capitalists to keep people divided. He said that by their separating people of different races, the people would not unite and stand up to our own government to demand justice. He said racism benefited the capitalists and that it helped keep them in power.

I really enjoyed it when the Party had meetings at our home. I would wander in and out of the meetings, catching a few interesting discussions. Then, as I grew older, I listened more closely. I learned a lot about the class struggle, racism, and problem-solving skills. I remember one time when I was twenty-three and they were talking about how to get people involved in the struggle. I recall speaking out and saying they were using guilt on people and I didn't think people move out of guilt. And I remember some of the members looked at me with respect for my bringing up that point. A comrade said, "She makes sense. Let's look at that, maybe we do use guilt."

Unlike my siblings, I did not enjoy our traveling to the San Luis Valley. We had to go over the old La Vita Pass with narrow, winding roads. I always succeeded in getting carsick. So of course the other kids fussed about that. There were six of us in the car, and we were all crowded, and by the time we arrived at our Grandma's house, I was a wreck.

What I did enjoy on the long trip was listening to my parents sing and harmonize to a song in Spanish, "Soy Un Pobra Venadito" (I'm a Poor Little Deer). That particular song made me feel happy that my parents loved each other a lot.

Soy Un Pobre Venadito
Soy un pobre venadito que habito en la sierrania
Soy un pobre venadito que habito en la sierrania
Como no soy tan mancito no abajo al agua de dia.

I'm a poor little deer
I'm a poor little deer that lives in the mountains
I'm a poor little deer that lives in the mountains
Because I'm not so tamed I don't come down for the water by day—
At night little by little into your arms I come (love) of mine.

Every so often, when our father could afford it, we were treated to a great hamburger deluxe in a restaurant. Us kids would steal the little coffee cream. Boy was it good! That was the thrill of my life.

Dad always took bags of groceries to his mother, Grandma Marina's, house. He told us that we couldn't go without taking food. That instilled in me not to ever impose on people.

It was great once we got there. Aunt Odila, Dad's sister who was my favorite aunt during my childhood, always had fresh baked pies and bread for us. I just loved the smell in their kitchen and the hugs that went along with the welcome. I loved all my cousins and really enjoyed playing with them. We talked and laughed in bed till the wee hours of the morning.

When I became a teenager we were allowed to go to the dances in the San Luis Valley and dance with the guys. We even got to buy new dresses for these special occasions. The fiestas were called Santiago and Santa Ana. And I loved getting attention from the country guys.

My brother, Richard (Patrick), is the youngest child in our family. Here is his take on life in our family:

I was born in 1947, in Denver, Colorado, the only child of my parents born in a hospital. I was born into a large family of five boys and four girls.

My mother had miscarried before she had me. While she was pregnant with me, she had to go to the hospital every day so the doctors could keep close watch over her. I was the ninth and youngest child of Roberto and Edna Trujillo. We are a Mexican-American family.

When I was four years of age, I used to run and jump on the back of cable cars that ran in front of our house. I would ride them down Tejon Street about four blocks, where I would get off and walk back home. My mother was the disciplinarian, and she got a limb from the lilac tree to whip me. It was quite a whipping, and I never rode that cable car again. My father never hit me no matter what I did, but my mother sure did.

On my first day of kindergarten, my sister Mary Lou took me to class, and all I could do was cry and ask her to please not leave me there. Well anyway, after that first day I really enjoyed school because I was able to play with my sisters at school.

At home I grew up with my sisters Orlanda, Rena, and Mary Lou. Orlanda is nine years older than I, Rena is seven years older, and Mary Lou is five years older than I am. They were responsible for teaching me how to be the best dancer. I could dance the stroll, the swing, the cha cha, and the Latino soul. I didn't have as deep a relationship with my older siblings because we were so far apart in age.

Belonging to a Mexican (Latino) family was the best! The food was outrageously good. We had fresh bread or fresh tortillas daily. We had menudo, enchiladas, green chile, beans, potatoes, and tamales. Dad had rabbits in a barn behind our house. Sometimes we had 200 rabbits. We were always eating rabbit meat, and it was excellent!

Dad would go to the farms and bring back lambs, pigs, calves, and chickens and slaughter them right in an old barn. I recall watching him gut them, skin them, cut them into pieces, in awe that my father knew how to do everything!

Later I found out that he had brought up seven of my brothers and sisters during the Great Depression, which was a feat in itself. He used to tell us stories about how they suffered in those times. He was a survivalist to have gone through those difficult times.

I recall my growing-up years being filled with a lot of playing: cowboys and Indians, Zorro, Superman, marbles. Gosh, my mother was forever putting patches on my jeans. One time I was being Superman and Zorro at the same time. I put on my black Zorro cape (a big black raincoat), and I climbed the garage roof, and I positioned myself to fly, and I shut my eyes, took a deep breath, and jumped off the garage roof! Something went wrong! I didn't fly like Superman and Zorro. I fell pretty hard and broke my arm. Boy, I was always in trouble!

The next important event in my life was when my sister Mary Lou got married. I was so happy, sad, and lonely. She was going to Killeen, Texas, with her husband, Virgil, who was in the army. I was so traumatized when she left that I ran after the train they were on to the end of the platform crying my heart out, not that we always got along so well, because we were always torturing each other. But I wouldn't have anyone to tease any more.

After my sister Mary Lou left, I was the only child left at home. At the time, my father owned his own construction-cement business, and he was working long hours, and it was very hard work. At the age of fifteen I worked for him until I started college. He paid me very good wages.

Anyway, he was doing very well financially in the small construction business and he was able to treat me better financially than the older kids because he had the means to do so. Whereas he couldn't do that for his other kids because of the depression and the few jobs he had.

On my twelfth birthday, in 1959, my parents bought me a beautiful bike. With that bike I started working delivering newspapers both in the mornings before school and in the afternoons. I made around $300.00 a month. I always had money in my pocket. In addition to that, I used to go to bingo all the time and I'd win $150.00 sometimes. So I was doing pretty well for a fifteen-year-old.

We grew up in a fun neighborhood. I had a wonderful childhood. Across the street was a potato-chip factory where they made everything fresh daily. They had potato chips, chile chips, and shoestring potato chips. Right next door to the factory was a pie shop where we could buy a split banana cream pie for eighty cents. Then we even had a popcorn company in the middle of the block where they had regular and cheese popcorn, caramel corn, candy, and beef jerky. Then there was the Marigold Restaurant on the corner, which had the best authentic Italian cuisine in town. Then two blocks down we had the famous Gaetano's Restaurant. It was all a guy could do to stay skinny.

I used to hang out mostly with Mexicans, a few Italians, and a Polish guy was my best friend. As I got older, I had a few Black friends. I was brought up with no prejudiced views. I recall my father telling people he wouldn't mind if I fell in love with an Indian woman or a nice Black woman. He wanted us to be an international, multicultural family.

We took many trips to the San Luis Valley when I was a child. And I remember having some wonderful times. On my mother's side, we visited her sister, Reina, and her husband, Adolph, and my cousin Tita. Mom also had a brother, my Tio (uncle) Juanito, and his wife, Claudita. They owned a little store, and my Tio always gave me candies and pop. I loved the country. It was so beautiful, and there were no people around. I used to go horseback riding, fishing, or just walking around looking for arrowheads. I used to find a lot of them.

On my father's side, he had four sisters: Odelia, Della, Madeline, and Frances and my Grandma, Marina. She was the only grandparent I ever knew. She was very old, around eighty-years-old, but to me she looked one hundred.

As a child my favorite activity was to go camping and fishing with my Mom and Dad. We would get away to the mountains nearly every weekend in the summertime. We went to Pitkin, Colorado, near

Gunnison, where Mom and Dad lived when they first got married and Dad used to be a logger. We enjoyed fishing all of Colorado and much of Wyoming, and we even fished in Yellowstone National Park. Mom, Dad, and I were expert fishermen. These times are the happiest memories of my life.

When I was thirteen-years-old, my father bought a brand new 1959 Ford. I was delivering the *Rocky Mountain News* in the wintertime, and it was 26 below zero. Soon after Dad bought the new car, I got in the car because Dad had left it parked in the driveway. I started the car to drive it into the garage for him. Instead of putting on the brakes to stop the car, I accidentally stepped on the gas and I took that car right through the garage! The car was wrecked and the bricks were all broken down on the car and everywhere. Boy, was I scared! My dad was really mad at me. I can still remember him yelling at me.

Then, around the same age, Dad and Mom took me to Old Mexico for a whole month. We drove through Texas in order to see my sister Mary Lou and my brother-in-law Virgil, in Killeen, Texas. My sister had just had a baby girl. It was so wonderful to see them and my new niece.

We proceeded on to Mexico and went through Monterrey and San Luis Potosi before arriving in Mexico City, where we stayed for two weeks. I remember it well. There was a lot of poverty and a lot of homeless people. People were sleeping outdoors and begging us for money. If I remember right, there were 500,000 people living in a shantytown next to the city dump. We visited the university and many museums and ate a lot of good food.

Then we were off to Acapulco, Mexico. It was an eight-hour drive through the mountains. We stopped in a city named Taxco that was in the middle of the mountains, and it was a silver-mining village, and they had beautiful jewelry and blankets for sale. The cobblestone streets were very narrow and steep. It was a very unique little town. In Acapulco we rented a room on a cliff next to the sea. When we looked down from the balcony, it was a straight drop to the sea. It was absolutely beautiful. The food was excellent. We ate a lot of fresh seafood and fresh fruit every morning that I had never eaten before, like papaya and some different foods. For me, at thirteen-years-old, I was full of energy and hormones. I would go to the beach at 3:00 in the morning and go swimming by the full moon, all by myself.

I went to a bullfight with my parents, and after the first bull was killed, my parents left because they couldn't take the mistreatment and torture the bull was put through. I stayed to see the end of the bullfight. I also saw cock fights, which is also a lot of torture to animals. But I also saw a lot of wonderful things! I saw the cliff beavers. I saw marlin, giant turtles, whales, and porpoise. We went on a yacht cruise with a couple of New Yorkers and Puerto Ricans that Mom and Dad had made friends with. They had mariachi music on board. And I was fetching drinks for everyone, and in the process I would get one for myself. This was my first experience with drinking.

Years later in 1986, one month after the Chernobyl nuclear accident near Kiev, Russia, I went on a five-city tour of Russia (then the Soviet Union) with my sister Orlanda and my brother-in-law Gil. We were scheduled to visit Kiev, but they changed our itinerary to visit Minsk, Russia, instead. We were there for twenty-eight days and visited the cities of Leningrad. Minsk, Yalta, Krasnador, and Moscow. While I was there, Russia was still a socialist country. From my experience there, I saw that they still had a class society, with the upper class much better off than the working and poor classes.

In general, I think that when people are given power, they seem to take advantage of it and become corrupt. Russia itself was extremely beautiful and enchanting, with a rich historical past. I very much loved the country, and the people were very friendly. On the other hand, the technology, sewer systems, medical care, and living conditions were very backward and inadequate. But I had to remember that I was comparing that country with the richest country in the world, the United States.

My husband, Virgil, writes: "I met Mary Lou in 1957 at a dance club in south Denver. My first impression of her was that she made me feel like a man. I was twenty-one-years-old and later I found out she was only fifteen. She seemed much older than her years, and she had a lot of class, and she was very beautiful. I felt weak and unsure of myself. I didn't have much self-confidence at the time because we were poor and I was raised on a farm in the San Luis Valley. It had only been a year since we had moved to Denver. So this city girl was very attractive to me, and I couldn't believe she actually liked me.

I fell in love with Mary Lou even before I knew anything about her. She was still in high school, and I am almost seven years older than she is. But I knew right away that I wanted to marry her and spend the rest of my life with her. She said I was crazy, because I didn't even know her. But I knew that I wanted her to be my wife.

We started dating, and I brought her home to meet my parents, and they found out her parents were also from the San Luis Valley. My relatives who lived in Denver knew that Robert Trujillo was a communist, and they told my parents and, of course, my family tried talking to me about not getting too serious with this girl. Because they were taught to think communists were evil, they were concerned about me being involved with that kind of life. They did not trust communists because they didn't understand them, and because Mary Lou's father was a communist, they were afraid. See, everything I ever learned in the Catholic Church, the schools, and my own family was against communism. I was taught that all communists were evil, that they were devils. I was not to trust them because they wanted to overthrow our government and bring us under a dictatorship. And if they succeeded in overthrowing our government, we would all be put in concentration camps. I remember as a young boy when they rounded up the Japanese people in the San Luis Valley and took them off to camps.

I had already fallen for her, and it didn't matter to me who her father was. Anyway, we didn't even know what a communist was. In fact we didn't even know what capitalism meant or how it works. We just bought into everything that was taught [socialized] to us and we didn't question anything about our system.

Then all my family are Republicans, so they weren't about to accept a communist!

Sorry! I was already crazy in love with Mary Lou, and that was the end of any discussion about it. Two years later I married the enemy, the daughter of a communist! We got married in June of 1959, and I took her with me to Texas to finish out my time in the Army. A year and a half later we had our first child there. Our daughter was born in an army hospital.

After my discharge, we came back to Denver with our new baby girl, and we bought a home a block away from her parents. That's when I started listening to her father and her family's discussions about politics, socialism, and communism. For several years I didn't like what I was hearing. They were talking about all the things I was taught to believe in, and they were against the injustices, but I felt that they were against everything I believed in. I was driving a bus at the time, and I would think for hours, as I was driving, about their talks, and at times I was confused and it all seemed too strange to me. Then I thought, "They make so much sense." It took me years to open my mind trying to understand.

After several years of listening, questioning and learning, and watching my father-in-law fight for justice, I learned more about the politics of our society and I respected him. He taught me a lot about politics, and over the years he became my best friend. When I really started to understand the way things work in our society, I joined my father-in-law and my wife in demonstrations against police brutality, the war in Vietnam, the Gulf War, and the farm workers' struggle. In 1997 my wife and I participated in the first World's Peace Conference for Children. It was called "Mothers of the Earth for World Peace Summit" in Vienna, Austria. We met Betty Williams, a leader of the people who are struggling for justice in Ireland, and Jean Houston, author and scholar in the United States.

Through the experiences of family members, the common thread that ran throughout each of our lives: the commitment to love, peace, and justice. We have our parents' teachings and their living example of these values. As children growing up, one of the most important values my dad taught us was to struggle for justice through non-violence. He believed he could change the world without violence; therefore, he expected us to resolve conflict through dialogue, organization, and peaceful demonstration. Dad led by example, showing us time and again how to create change, understanding, and persuasion, through peaceful means. He taught us that poverty, racism, injustice, and war are all forms of violence.

Dad's fear and anger about the injustices moved him to action. Robert was a humanitarian, a follower of Christ and a communist. His fear, anger, and love were the sparks that gave fuel to his passion to help create a just world.

Chapter 7

Fear/Anger/Love

At the risk of seeming ridiculous, the true revolutionary is guided by deep feelings of love.

Che Guevara

The other side of love is anger/hate, and under anger is often fear. Robert was very angry about inequalities and injustices. His stored-up anger energy was controlled rage, which he used most effectively by releasing his anger in a powerful manner at public meetings, at rallies, in letters to representatives and members of Congress, and to the media. He got people to listen, and, whether they agreed with him or not, he held their attention. He was charismatic, and the power of his words made him very effective. He had an extraordinary mind along with the art of clarity. His insight, hindsight, and foresight came from his clear thinking. Seldom have I heard such an eloquent speaker.

It never failed to amaze me how he read through everything and everyone. He was able to see clearly the underlying motives in any person, policy, or situation. For example, he saw through the false airs, the games people play, and what he called "wrong intentions," which he explained as unduly selfish motives of individuals. Yet he always excused individuals on the grounds that they were products of the system and that they were socialized to be that way. His criticism was directed more towards the system and its leaders and representatives than towards the individual. For the most part I believe he saw the leaders as overpowering the individuals, who in their powerlessness were not questioning the leaders. I differ in my opinion, because I believe both leaders and individuals should be accountable for their actions and behavior.

Within our family, he seemed to know when one of the kids wasn't telling the truth.

He had a way that must have affected us heavily, because the truth always seemed to come out. Then it was worse because then we had to be accountable for it.

He spoke of politicians to *Denver Post* staff writer Leonard Larsen:

> "Of course politicians will throw mud at each other when the campaign comes, but it's only one muddy face throwing mud at another muddy face." Larsen asked "If President Johnson were voted out of the White House, who would you suggest then?" "That's a good question," Robert answered. "It's like an individual. You marry a girl and she's unfaithful to you, who do you marry next, another unfaithful one maybe? You keep trying until you give up. That's why a lot of people refuse to vote today. Millions of people won't go to the polls anymore. It's nobody's fault but the politicians who don't keep their promises. [14]

It was as if everyone else just saw a beautiful table, but Robert would imagine the raw material: the tree the wood came from, and the tree being cut down, the entire process of making the table. He paid special attention to the labor that was put into creating and manufacturing the table. He would then see and compare the discrepancy between the wages of the workers and the profits of the owners.

I remember him attacking the diamond industry, explaining that the masses of people in South Africa who mine the

---

[14]   (Larsen, "Denver Communist 'Struggles' On," *The Denver Post*, 15 October, 1967.

diamonds were starving. He added that, in the society of apartheid, the 95% of the Black population of that country was controlled and ruled by the 5% White, wealthy people. He was very critical of the many people buying diamonds while, as he explained it, a third of the world was dying of malnutrition. He was upset even to the point of anger that people seemed to have little concern for those suffering in poverty.

There was a fine line between his anger and his fear. Actually anger was the cover up for his fear. He feared that if people did not struggle for peace, there would be World War III. He feared that President Ronald Reagan would continue to invade smaller Central American countries and continue to lie to cover up those acts around the globe, as the administration clearly was doing at that time with the Iran-Contra scandal.

He feared that institutional racism, compounded by the corruption of the higher political leaders, would continue. He feared that people's sense of powerlessness would continue and that the struggle against poverty and racism would stall. He feared that the wide use and abuse of drugs, brought into this country and other countries by the rich, would increase violence. He explained that drugs were being brought in for profit and to control and oppress the youth's natural minds, to stop them from getting involved in the struggle against these problems and against the capitalist system. He knew that as the use and abuse of drugs continued to spread, crimes would also increase. His youngest son had been arrested because of a DUI and possession of marijuana. So his fears were very close to his heart.

His anger surfaced in 1975, when his twenty-three-year-old grandson, Frank Trujillo Jr., was murdered at the Ware House nightclub during a performance of the B.B. King show. A complete stranger, after he and Frank had bumped into each other, called Frank Jr. a dirty Mexican. And Frank called him down. The man pulled a knife and stabbed Frank Jr. five times in the heart. Frank's parents never saw him alive again. When they arrived at the hospital, he was dead. The man who killed him was the son of a rich, White man who owned a chain of hotels in Cheyenne, Wyoming, and his wealth was able to buy his son out of the crime. My brother, Frank Sr., spent over $10,000 to bring this man to prison for killing his son. But the man's family had more money, and this travesty was the "justice" our family received. Frank Jr.'s life was over at twenty-three, and justice escaped the Trujillo family.

Our family and many supporters held a press conference at Our Lady of Guadalupe Hall to expose and protest this horrible crime and the injustice of its aftermath. Our press release stated, "If a poor Mexican had killed a White person, under the same conditions, the Mexican would serve a life sentence or be put to death." The girlfriend of the man who killed Frank Jr. and a member of the B.B. King band were put on the stand as witnesses to the murder. The girlfriend broke down hysterically, crying in the courtroom and saying that her boyfriend (the rich man's son) had stabbed Frank Jr. in the heart and that she saw it happen. She said she could not remain silent any longer because she was not sleeping. So she told the truth, but even with her testimony, the man got off scot-free after committing murder.

How did this happen? It's the way money has always been a leading factor in who gets sentenced for a crime and who gets set free. The reason given for the man's acquittal was that authorities could not find the murder weapon. Therefore, we can conclude that one can murder another person and discard the weapon and get away with murder if one is wealthy. I do not think this would be the case if the murderer had been a poor Mexican or Black or any other poor person.

The day after Frank was murdered, my mother was rushed to the hospital with chest pains, and the following day my younger brother was arrested for possession of marijuana. I received a call from the jail, and I hated to tell my father. I took him for a walk and we held hands as I told him about the call. He responded by saying "Hija, as long as we have love for each other, we have a reason to live. We will get your brother out of jail and get him help. It is too late for us to help our Frankie, but we can still help your brother," and he broke down crying.

Michael S. Cummings, a University of Colorado at Denver professor, interviewed Robert just before he died in 1985. He asked him, "What things have caused you the most personal pain you have had to cope with in your life?" And Robert replied, "The worst was when a priest, Father Jose Lara, and my daughter, Mary Lou, came in the early morning to tell us that Frankie Trujillo Jr. [our Grandson] was murdered. That was the worst shock of my life."

The way Robert coped with his pain over losing his grandson was to continue his life's path to create justice. In 1978 he was one of twenty participants in a Hunger Strike showing support for Chileans who had mysteriously disappeared. He participated in demonstrations and continually wrote letters to the representatives to try to influence them in their decisions. [15]

1978, A Hunger Strike:

In 1978 reporter Karen Newman wrote in *The Rocky Mountain-News:*

About 20 persons participated in a hunger strike at St. Dominic Catholic Church to show "solidarity" with Chileans who said friends and relatives have disappeared since a military regime took over that country in 1973.

Wednesday night, according to the Associated Press, nearly 100 Chileans ended their seventeen-day strike in churches in Santiago. Some of the strikers were taking glucose by the time the fast ended and most were expected to remain in the churches for a few days in order to begin walking and eating gradually.

The Santiago strike ended after Roman Catholic bishops were told the Chilean government intended to provide information about the missing persons.

A year ago, government promises of information about the missing persons ended a similar hunger strike in Santiago, but strikers at St. Dominic's Thursday said those promises were not kept.

The strikers, representing various religious and political groups, assembled at St. Dominic's Thursday morning for a press conference before the strike was to begin.

---

[15]   [See Robert's letters in Appendix, p. 181.]

Robert Trujillo, representing the Colorado Communist party, wept as he promised the group that, although he is 75 years old, he [would] participate in the hunger strike.

"I am willing… to stay all night and not close my eyes to protest what's happening in Chile. I'll stay with you here," Trujillo said.[16]

Robert wrote a TV announcer at KCNC, Channel 4 the following letter:

December 19, 1983

"Dear Mr. Bob Palmer:

In response to your Saturday night newscast, where you asked listeners to take [their turn] in regard to the issue of the danger of a nuclear war, I want to express myself in hope that you will read my letter on your Channel 4 TV newscast.

It must torture the minds of many listening to President Ronald Reagan's rhetoric about the need of more and more weapons to "Protect the freedoms of the American people" from the Russians. Today, December 19, 1983 in the Rocky Mountain News, Reagan uses the Bible to defend his foreign policy of a nuclear war—Armageddon—to carry on his plans to get our nation involved in a war with the Soviet Union. One could say that Ronald Reagan has gone completely crazy if his policy was not so dangerous to the world.

But this attempt to continually lie about the Soviet Union as being the "Threat to Peace" is trying to cover up the causes of all the problems in the capitalist world by blaming the Soviet Union. The Soviet Union has no unemployment, no racial oppression, and no homeless people! Why does capitalism have these problems and cannot solve them? The Soviet Union lost 20 million people when Hitler invaded that nation. They want no war! Let capitalism and socialism compete in a peaceful way.

---

[16]   Karen Newman, "1978 A Hunger Strike," *The Denver Post*, Fri., 9 June. 1978.

If Christ comes to run the world with "Justice and Peace" after a nuclear war, as some "preachers" claim, there will be nothing left but a huge pile of ashes.

Peace.
Robert Trujillo

The desire to effect change was utmost in Robert's mind. He found many ways in which to try to do so, and if he could not take a stand by speaking out, he wrote to newspaper journals, TV announcers, or whomever he could find to voice his outrage over injustices.

Anger, fear, and love were motivating factors throughout Dad's life. Nothing kept him from action. His courage, determination, and conviction, although admirable, did not make for an easy life, and I often try to understand why he took this difficult road.

Chapter 8

Reflection and Analysis

During the first five years of Robert's life, his formative years, he was brought up with strong religious teachings. He was taught that if one suffers in this life, he would be rewarded in the hereafter. His deep religious convictions from childhood were transformed into deep social convictions in his adult life.

Transformation

Robert's connection with the Catholic religion instilled in him some of the beliefs and values of the Catholic Church and Christ's teachings. I recall him saying to us kids,

"You cannot serve two Gods: God and wealth." He was referring to the first of the Ten Commandments, which forbids us to put anything before God. But I'm sure Dad was more concerned with not putting wealth before service to the poor. He taught us that gossip was a waste of energy that we should be using to educate ourselves and contribute our life to making the world better. He did not believe in killing and advocated nonviolence. That value came from the commandment. "Thou shalt not kill." Like Christ, Robert believed in justice and devoted his life's work towards that aim. As Jesus was a friend of the poor, so was Robert.

Robert not only believed in these values but also tried his best to practice them. Yet the commandment "Thou shalt not steal" was not one that Robert kept during the Depression. He and others had stolen coal to warm their homes in the cold winters. After he lost his job, he went to the Catholic priest for support, and the priest told him that the economic crash was the will of God and that the church could not help him. Robert didn't agree, and he continued his quest for justice. He stopped going to church and started organizing the unemployed. Eventually he stopped believing in a religious God and rejected organized religion altogether. But he remained a humanitarian. In my analysis, he merely transferred his belief in God and heaven to his new belief in socialism and communism.

Socialization influences from the early political socialization process are extremely important, and in fact many times they remain so throughout a person's life. Such was the case with Robert. This is not to say that changes in awareness do not continue in adult life, but that early political beliefs are the most resistant to change in later life. Both Plato and Rousseau, in their concern for producing good citizens, paid close attention to what a child experiences during the early years.[17]

It appears that in Robert's case, his early political beliefs were formed from learning values such as sharing, responsibility, and sacrifice that he received from his home and family, the Catholic Church, and his culture. These values were similar to those of socialism and were in part resistant to change in his later years. He took his values and principles with him when he made the transition to a belief in socialism.

Religious teaching, on the one hand, conditions the mind to resist injustices and, on the other hand, advocates that suffering be endured as the will of God. As these two opposing forces were at work in Robert's mind, something happened over time that created change in him. Robert used to say, "If we practice what we learn from our religion, then we must identify with all of humanity. I can only do this by being politically involved." He felt that where there were injustices, one had to take a political stand to expose and change them. It just

---

[17]   *[See Mary Lou Salazar, Master's thesis, *Political Socialization in Cuba in the Area of Education*, 1982, at The University of Colorado, Boulder, Norland Library stacks, call # T 1982.Sa 31.]

so happened that the results that the church counts on to create the position that supports both the church and the larger society (such as unquestioned patriotism), in Robert's case created unintended results. He tried to follow the values he had learned from his religion and instead became an advocate against the church and capitalist society. It seems as if in Robert's mind becoming a revolutionary was closer to the teachings of Christ than were the doctrines of the church and the political system. For instance, "thou shalt not kill." but if you are called to war, you may well have to kill another human being. He resolved this contradiction by resisting injustices throughout his life and becoming a peaceful revolutionary.

No Political Butterfly

Robert was no political butterfly, as Tom Gavin wrote in *The Denver Post* on March 3, 1986, about Robert, after his death. "He became a Communist and he remained one. Robert Trujillo was no political butterfly and was bulldog stubborn." Robert was very stubborn about keeping the values he had been taught in the church. It was these values that he found were in concert with those of the Communist Party. It was the teachings of Christ that fit nicely with socialism.

It interested me to learn while I was researching the Penitentes religious sect that they were involved in the political arena of the San Luis Valley. It seems to me that Robert was influenced by their work even though he may not have been consciously aware of this influence in his early development. The Penitentes were involved in the political arena of the communities. As children, we pick up a lot of information, and the brain is a mass computer, storing information in our subconscious mind.

There was structure in the Communist Party as well as in the Catholic religion that made the transition from one to the other easy for Robert. Therefore, I saw the transformation from the institution of the Catholic Church to the Communist Party as a smooth transition for him, despite the "tough life" noted by Tom Gavin in *the Denver Post* on June 26, 1985. Gavin did not see Robert's life as an easy one: "Robert Trujillo has been so concerned about social ills that he has his entire adult life swum upstream, politically, at who knows what personal cost. You don't attain ease and plenty by being a public communist in a state like Colorado, or any other American State I can think of."

As I recall from my science studies, the pregnant fish swam upstream to deposit their eggs and the ones that made it grew fins in the process. I think Robert had some pretty big fins!

The ideology and structure in the Communist Party promotes the political action so crucial to getting the Party's work accomplished. Robert believed that heaven (being socialism) would come to this earth but that the people had to work to make that happen. He thought that under socialism life would be free of exploitation, insecurity, and deprivation. He believed in the creation of a truly humane and rational society that would allow the development of the fullest potential of the human being. He used to tell me, "Hija, heaven and hell are right here on earth." As a communist he rejected the idea of the supernatural and rejected all static concepts of reality. He replaced his belief in God with recognition that social change is fundamental, and his faith was directed towards building socialism.

In fact I do not think Robert would have been devastated by the collapse of the Soviet Union. Because he told me once that, if it ever happened that the Soviet Union did not work for the good of all people, then the people there would just have to struggle to replace it with something better. He truly saw the flaws of mankind, yet he was also aware of man's potential for good. In Marxist theory, "Dialectical Materialism explains the world, not as a complex of ready-made things, but as a complex of processes, in which all things go through uninterrupted change of coming into being and passing away."[18]

Robert was an agnostic or, better yet, a humanist. I knew Robert as a man who believed deeply in brotherhood and sisterhood. I knew his soul. And to me a man that cared so much

---

[18]   Maurice Cornforth, *Materialism and the Dialectical Method*, (New York; International Publishers, 1971.)

for a better world for all humanity had to have God's power within.

Another important aspect of Robert's character was his commitment to his values. The Communist Party demanded commitment as well as discipline, responsibility, and hard work. Likewise, commitment to God and the teachings of the church, which teaches discipline and responsibility, are expected from the good Christian, as is the hard work that is essential to becoming a good person. Robert was a hard worker, superior in his capacity for achievement and pushing his cause to the limits.

There was also the element of passion so visible in Robert and the members of the Party. An illustration of this kind of passion is described in the book *The Romance of American Communism* by Vivian Gomick, 1977. The following are excerpts from a personal interview with a doctor who had left the Communist Party. Dr. Rindzer states:

> "So for me there's no politics anymore. The years when I was a Communist bar none, were the best years of my life. The relationship for me between the personal and the historical was intense, deeply felt, fully realized. Now, I live an entirely personal life, removed from the larger world. I feel no interest in anything beyond my work. I work hard, I'm proud of the work I do, I consider it an obligation to take as much responsibility for the medical profession as I can, but that's it. The world is smaller, colder, darker by far for me than it was when I was a Communist... That's a funny thing to say here, isn't it?" He laughs, waving his hand toward the brilliant Arizona afternoon. "I've made my peace with my life, but I have no illusions that I live a life of larger meaning."

Robert had the kind of passion illustrated by Dr. Rinzer when he was a Communist. In fact Robert's passion to create a better world was a motivating factor in his forcefulness in the struggle toward socialism. Robert also found joy in the wonders of life. For example, when I first started college, I was telling him about the layers of the earth below the surface, and I illustrated the layers by drawing an onion. He got excited like a child and said, "There are just too many things to learn about and so many things we just don't understand. No matter how long we live, we cannot learn everything." He loved knowledge. It was one of his passions. I know that he would have been an outstanding scholar, if he had had the opportunity to go to college. And without a doubt his greatest passion was being a communist to help build a better world.

Robert loved nature and was most at home when he was out in the wilderness fishing and camping. He was a great fisherman, and he, my mother, and my younger brother and at times other family members spent weekends enjoying time outdoors. It was great fun.

Robert's life had many inner conflicts, and he often shared his dreams with me. He was very emotional, and his dreams represented that aspect of his inner struggle. When I would share my analysis of some of his dreams or tell him my interpretations of some of my dreams, he didn't want to hear my interpretation. One time, I told him that at times guilt comes from the Catholic teachings and his father's being a Penitente must have affected him in this area. I mentioned sexual guilt to him that I suspect he had because of all the religious teachings, around carnal sin. He just listened but made no comment.

In my study of Gandhi, I saw similarities between Gandhi and my Dad. Like Gandhi Robert was taught that every natural feeling is a sin. And like Gandhi, Robert adored his mother. Robert, also like Gandhi, believed in non-violence. And like Gandhi, Robert was a revolutionary.[19]

Alienation

Did Robert feel alienated? He must have at times because his mother and sisters and most of his relatives did not share

---

[19]   *Gandhi All Men Are Brothers: Autobiographical Reflections,* (Columbia University Press 1958.) and Louis Fisher, *The Life of Mahatma Gandhi,* (Harper and Brothers, 1950.)

his belief in communism. All of his children except for Gil respected and understood his commitment to communism, and we all knew that he made sense because many of his views and predictions fit the real world. Yet none of us took as big a risk as he did. I know I didn't, but I'm a chip off the old block, and I have a fighting spirit of my own. And placed in a situation like another Depression when we all lose our jobs as my father did during the Great Depression, I know exactly what I would do. I'd organize the people and demand jobs.

Robert struggled with personal relationships with his siblings, his children, and at times my mother. There were many people who did not like my father for his beliefs and strong character. Many times, he would dominate conversations, and I would say he seemed at times fanatic in his desire to sway people towards socialism.

Anger is a learned behavior. Poverty creates anger, despair, and hopelessness. Economic injustice causes poverty. Poverty, in many cases, produces guilt, shame, hurt, fear, anger, and long-term frustration and rage, and in many cases the results are illness, crime, and violence. Therefore, poverty is violence!

Robert directed his hurt, anger, frustration, and rage in the direction of trying to bring justice to the world. He was very angry because his two baby brothers had died of malnutrition. He felt that their lives would have been saved if the family had not been poor. I don't think he ever got over that tragedy. In fact, whenever he read of people dying of starvation, it would really affect him. He felt rage at every injustice he saw or heard about throughout his life.

Because he was the eldest child and only son in his family, he was expected to take on the role of provider for his family beginning when he was sixteen years old. His role of responsibility led him into the political arena during the Depression. And he took the path that he felt would help reduce the suffering. I'm sure he felt resentment at times over having so many burdens to carry. He surely carried his cross.

I've tried to figure out how Robert kept the faith, with opposition everywhere around him. He had a number of very close "comrade friends" in Denver. He was connected to his work, believing in socialism with every bit of his being. He worked at different jobs, but his commitment to communism and to the building of it was never shaken. He had a deep and loving relationship with his wife, although they had their share of challenges. They certainly had differences, but love, loyalty, friendship, and shared values prevailed.

Robert was closely connected with the poor and the working class. He never moved out of his North Denver home, where he served the poor for years. His door was always open to family, friends, and strangers. He counseled neighbors, he loved his raza (people), but he didn't care what race, religion, or class people came from: if they needed help, he gave it. He was a notary, and his license helped him to get people into his home. And after he had listened empathically to their problems, he gave them suggestions and direction on where to go for help or what to do. For instance, he sent a young woman to the welfare office after he had called a senator to complain about this woman's situation, of her not getting her checks on time. He also helped her apply for food stamps. After such interactions, he would explain how the system of capitalism operates and he would give people the communist paper, *The Daily World,* to try to educate them in the direction of socialism.

Robert had a special but different relationship with each one of his children. They all knew in their own way that he loved them, and he knew how much they each loved him. But I'm sure he was alienated from his son Gil, and I'm sure Gil was alienated from him. The two of them were worlds apart in their political beliefs. But like Robert, Gil went back and forth between being an atheist and an agnostic. Like Robert, Gil was very stubborn and was very rebellious.

In some ways I feel that my husband, Virgil, helped fill the void for Dad and also for Mom over the loss of their son Gil. Over the years, my husband and my dad became best friends, but their relationship did not come without conflict. They were alike in ways: some of their old habits of "machismo" came up time and again, and they clashed. Their relationship improved after their initial conflict, and I know they learned from each other's virtues and flaws. They respected each other better after arguing over their differences about me. They each wanted to control me. And I rebelled against both of them to become my own person. They were fishing buddies; in fact my husband never went fishing again after my father passed away. They played cards on holidays and shared many special times together. They also confided in one another, and Robert taught my husband cement work.

I had a very special relationship with my dad, one that I still miss. He spent many hours at Virgil's and my home. Dad knew well how much my family and I loved him. Each of my children loved and respected their grandfather, and he, in turn, was loving, stem, and proud of them. Dad and I were very close. Intellectually, we had many inspiring encounters. He would tell me stories about his family, and his sister, Della, who then was ninety-four, she told me she wondered why her brother was so angry as a young man. I explained to her. "He was only sixteen-years-old when your father died, and he had to quit school, which he loved. He was saturated in grief over the loss of his father and sister. Then he had to leave home to be a shepherd, and he was responsible for raising all you girls. Plus, when he married and had a large family, the Depression hit. How would you feel?" She said. "Yes, I can see why he was so angry." My Aunt Della has only a daughter and a son, and even though she was raised in the same family, her life experience took her in a different direction from my father's.

During these conversations, Dad explained many things to me, and we would exchange views. He always gave me a lot of respect, as evidenced by his continuous eye contact and the way he listened to me with such interest. At times, I felt that I was teaching him something too. One time, I was explaining the theory of Marxism, and he said he wished he had gone to college because he hadn't learned all the theoretical concepts. But he really understood the practical; he lived and walked the talk. I used what I had learned from him and was many times ahead of other students applying that knowledge to my university studies.

From our talks, my father helped me to understand the nature of humanity and our imperfections as part of our being human. I feel that his own deep sense of caring was the other side of his alienation. He loved so deeply that he would get angry that others seemed not to care. This reaction may have also reflected his issue of control.

One time, he was watching the news with my mother, and they saw babies being burned with napalm in Vietnam. After a sleepless night, he woke up and decided to stop paying his taxes. He told Mom that his tax dollars were being used to kill people and babies, and he would not contribute to that horror. He never paid taxes after that, and after Dad passed away, his oldest son, Frank, had to pay back taxes to the IRS.

I felt his alienation when he struggled with a problem, and our long talks not only helped him but they helped me. I recall his close friend Roy, telling me once that whenever anyone in the Party criticized my father, he would agonize about it for days. He was a critic capable of self-criticism.

He worried about the problems in the world, and he worried about his own family. He worried about my back injuries (I was in two car accidents). He often told me that I'd better not die before him because he would not be able to bear that. He wanted to send me to the Soviet Union, where he felt the doctors could help me.

He loved his dog, Yo Yo, and his bond with that little dog was quite special. Robert is remembered in the neighborhood for walking his dog everyday. Yo Yo was in our family for thirteen years, and one day Dad hooked him to a steel post as he had done many times before while he took his car out of the garage. He backed up the car, and somehow Yo Yo got loose and Dad ran over his beloved little dog and killed him. Dad was devastated! He kept calling himself a murderer. It must have been a terrible nightmare for him because I felt he loved that dog as much as he loved his children. To add to his pain, it had only been a short time since he had lost his son Gil. Dad shared a recurring dream with me of Yo Yo calling for him to go with him. That loss for him was terribly painful. After it happened, he would walk over to our house, but he was never the same again. He was lost without his little buddy, Yo Yo. He seemed detached and alienated after that tragedy.

Around this time Dad's close friend and comrade Roy died. He told me after the memorial that everybody was dying. I would just listen to him consumed by his grief. Roy had been his friend for sixty years. It wasn't that everyone was dying; it was that those very close to him were dying.

The major influences that formed Robert's passionate search for justice were: a profound reverence for life, his desire for peace, and his path towards building socialism. Sacrifice was rooted in his home and family, his religion, culture, and tradition. His major guides were his mother and his wife, and his political development was tied closely to his religious teachings and the inequalities in America concerning the working class and the poor. He was affected by his exposure to the injustices of the poor. And last, but surely not least, were his involvement and leadership in the Communist Party, which enriched his life and gave him joy in serving the people. All the influences in his life experiences helped shape this unusual and charismatic man.

Robert's story reflects his many experiences. For instance, he was born into the working class. Poverty, ignorance, racism, and misery were his lot. I felt that in order to understand why he became a communist and remained one, it was necessary to examine his life through a historical perspective, including how others, especially family members, viewed him. Robert cared deeply, and he worked hard and long on his dream of creating a society with equitable distribution of wealth and greater well-being for humanity.

He once told me that in a master-slave society, the master, like the slave, is not free. He said, "The master spends his whole life trying to keep the slave from rebelling." He referred to the workers in the world as slaves of the capitalist. He touched many lives, and in turn many touched his life.

With respect and honor in the last year of his life, he was recognized and given a tribute for his lifelong work to bring better conditions for all people, especially the poor.

He lived a life of suffering and early in life subordinated his fun child, the joyful part of himself, cheating himself out of a lot of joy. This is not to say that he never experienced joy, because he did. He had many joyful moments, but for the most part, he remained very serious-minded, weighted down by the tremendous responsibilities he had assumed.

Chapter *9*

Tribute and Robert Trujillo's Last Interview

A year before my father died, family and friends gave my parents a tribute honoring them for a lifetime of service. It was held in the Community Center of Our Lady of Guadalupe Church, where close to two hundred people went to honor my parents for their contributions to peace and justice.

Henry Winston, National Chair of the US Communist Party came here from New York to be the honored guest speaker at a grand party to celebrate lifelong activists, Eduvijen (Edna) and Roberto Trujillo on March 30. [Winston passed away soon after Robert died in 1986], Gathering in the Community Center at Our Lady of Guadalupe Church, people came to honor the Trujillos. Present were many families from the Chicano community who have worked with Roberto on the various struggles affecting the lives of the workers here in Denver.

Testimonials were given and poems were read in English and Spanish that brought tears to our eyes. Among the people speaking were Mike Cummings, professor of political science here at University of Colorado at Denver; Jose Lara, longtime friend and political activist; as well as several members of the Trujillo family. From Arizona came Lorenzo Torrez, chair of the Chicano Commission of the CPUSA, Pat Bell/Blawis also came from Tucson to honor Roberto. People also came in from Salt Lake City, despite snowstorms, which covered our region. Letters were read from people who couldn't attend from Indiana and Connecticut. The Socialist Party sent a letter of congratulations.

Henry Winston spoke of how President Reagan would like to turn back the clock 50 years to undo the long hard struggles of community activists like Edna and Roberto Trujillo. Winston presented a plaque to the Trujillos. ["The Plaque read, "Robert has devoted his life to fighting racism, demanding full employment and creating peace and justice."] After the presentations, we pulled back the chairs and danced to the cumbias of the live band, Creation.

Roberto Trujillo has been a foundation for the Communist Party in Colorado and has devoted his life to fighting racism, demanding full employment and creating peace and justice in the world. When accepting the plaque to a standing ovation, Roberto told the gathering, "The highest honor anyone could give me and my wife is for people to continue and participate in the struggle for social justice, jobs and world peace." This truly reflects the workers' demands for peace, jobs, and justice."[20]

1985

I was asked to speak, and I read the poems I had written for my parents, bringing tears to their eyes.

I started:

"I mention Mother first, because beside every strong man is a strong woman, and sometimes women take a back seat to men, and yet it is those things that women give the world that keep the love rolling, the spirit moving, and the things that we need to survive".

"Their Life"

At 16 and 23 they married and vowed to love and be together for life.
Several children later, the Depression hit.

---

[20]   In 1985, LM, a staff writer for *The People's World* wrote: Trujillo Gets A 'Grand Party' L.M. staff writer for *The People's World*. 13 April 1985.

No food, no jobs, No Hope!
Years of struggle.
I questioned at times, what seemed real? —Their faith, their
love, their struggle to be free, left me born with a volcano in
me.
What did it do to the others, all of my sisters, all of my
brothers?

We too must struggle. We too must stand up for justice, for
peace, for love, for survival, for all the things that bring pur-
pose and meaning to life.
We never forget the memory of our beautiful Frankie and
how, over an argument, a man took his life, and our beautiful
brother, and son, Gil, who lives in all of us.

We too can't forget that to be passive is not man's true nature.
To be passive is not to care, for we are a part of and respon-
sible for the universal flight to create life, love, peace on earth
for all men, women, and children.

"Gratitude"

He will die in the spring, he will die in the fall, he will die in
the winter, the summer, he won't die at all.

What will I do after he dies? All the weak ones leave me
like flies. Who will teach us how to live, how to give, how
to truly understand the makeup of man, whom do I read my
poetry to?

Mary Lou, he'll always listen to you.
He will be by my side as life moves on with the tide.

Attitude of gratitude I feel today, my father is alive now and
through me he will always be.

Because men like him never die.
Women like me don't need to cry.

*I know there is no other. I still will have him in my brothers,
in my sisters, in my mother.*

*I'm so thankful I have my father, who art in my heart,
Long live Robert Trujillo, the hero of the poor, who taught us,*

*Life give us more,
Peace on earth,
Good will to men, be humanitarian,
Do all that you can.*

Robert and Edna

*The seeds that they planted continue to grow.
There're weeds that appear from the winters of their grief.
But the values of peace and friendship appear, as we watched
the Berlin Wall disappear.
The two world powers now willing to meet to reduce the arms
race.*

*At last we may see peace.
Where friends and families gather to share, where differences
don't matter when there's love in the air.*

*Thank you, our parents, for the love and the joy, for the values
of peace, of justice, of change.
The world is much better because you were here to teach
us some lessons that we all hold dear.*

*Your love was the greatest gift of them all... Your courage,
as well as your strength, your desire for truth, your fight till
the end,
gives us the courage never to bend.*

Your spirit lives on, in the mural on the wall.

**Ti doy la benedicion, Mom and Dad, from us all. *(I give you
the blessing)*

*Mary Lou Salazar
August, 1991*

My father's youngest sister, Frances, spoke at the celebration:

> One of the things I wish my brother would have left me was to have been a good speaker, like he was. But I am leaving that to his children.
>
> I am very happy to be here today because of my brother being honored, and I have always been very proud of him, even though we did not see eye to eye. But we had quite a few discussions, and he would always tell me. "What I like about you, Frances, is that you will listen to me and you give me back discussion, the others only listen." Well that is because I have always been a fighter, but in a different way.
>
> At least once a month I would go to the post office, and there was a real thick envelope with pictures and progressive articles underlined, and later, when we would see each other, we would discuss them. And he would tell me, "I know that, of all the people, you would be the only one to read them all."
>
> I asked Orlanda if I could speak today because, not only are we honoring my brother today, but I want from the bottom of my heart to honor his wife (who was such a good mother), and his children: his beautiful family that he loved and the love that this family has for my brother. As I sit here today and listen to all the kids, remember that they are my nieces and nephews, and I am so very proud of them honoring their father.

His Last Interview

In 1985, a year before Dad died, a man who had read an article on him in the local newspaper contacted him and asked if he could interview him. The man asked me not to use his name but gave me permission to use this interview:

The following are excerpts from the interview.

Listening to Trujillo, whose voice was strong and precise in spite of his eighty-one years, I was impressed with his clarity of expression in a man who had been a Catholic dropout.

His story was poignant, instilling in me an image of a man beyond and above the ordinary concept of the stereotyped communist. His experiences and hardships immediately dwarfed those in my own lifetime.

I began to see him as a fellow American and, maybe more to the point, as another human being struggling against extreme odds for his family's survival. He was a communist to be sure and in no way could I see myself making the kind of political decision he had made himself. Still, he was alerting me to a pressing need in our current American way of life. This had to do with a probable needful extension of personal preconceptions about people like Trujillo.

Here, at the very moment in history when Soviet and American governments are attempting some sort of sane approach to the insanity of nuclear warfare, I was being invited into a level of humanity I could positively identify with, even though it was coming from someone representing our avowed Enemy.

I did shed some tears later on, much to my surprise, in an interview with Trujillo's daughter, Mary Lou, when she had recalled memories and a love for her father. Perhaps even more so than her father, her two poems about her mom and dad touched me deeply because, unlike her dad, she is not a member of the Communist Party. She spoke as a daughter and with great reverence for what her father represents to her.

I was listening to people through feelings I could share with members of my own family. Then I found myself wondering about the progress of peace talks and about how added impetus might be given to them if more of us were exposed to the human essence in my friend's tape. At the conclusion I suggested this thought to my friend and he agreed that it may not be a bad idea at all if, with some editing Trujillo's and his daughter's versions of her interview could be shared by many other people. It was, so we both thought, worth a try."

The following are Robert's excerpts of the interview:

October, 1984

The early experiences in my life soon made me realize the injustices working people have to face in our kind of economy, the American way of life, or Reagonomics, where the government robs the people to pay the Pentagon.

Then, with readings in socialist literature and with a conviction that socialism was a more just economy for all the people, I joined the Communist Party. I worked hard to apply my newly found beliefs, and, years later, in 1961, my efforts were rewarded by my appointment to the Chairmanship of the Party in Colorado.

What I would like to impress people with is that the realities of life here soon strip away any illusions about justice for people who must earn their bread under the dictates of employers who are so often guided by the principles of profit and greed rather than by true concern for their fellow human beings. This inequality has grown so much, especially during the past decade, that people are afraid to walk the streets at night, afraid to leave their kids alone. Families seem to break down under these dehumanizing conditions. Thousands of kids flee from their homes and spend years in aimless wandering about the country looking for some kind of meaning in a life they find so difficult to understand. When they get a bit older, they become ripe for the drug merchants, and once again there is a waste of life, of true living experience, in frantic moods of escapism.

Many large farmers, especially in California, see more profit in raising marijuana then in growing food.

It is a very sad story we see unfolding here, and it continues, as long as there will be easy profits to be made. We don't have to look far for evidence of this. Right here in Denver in 1984 the signs of our social discrepancies are plain to see. Thousands of people in Denver are homeless and hungry, having to face severe winters in shelters, under bridges, in parked cars, and the like. I can't call this freedom. The extremes of too much wealth and too much poverty do not make freedom a reality. And these are not isolated statistics. Studies show that some 35 million Americans are living in poverty and there are at least 20 million hungry people in the United States of America.

I am now eighty-one years old, and I can say, in conclusion, that I doubt the ability of our capitalist system to go on breeding all of its ills without having to face a wall of opposition from so many people who have been hurt in so many unjust ways by a system that lacks true human values.

My father lived a difficult life, and he chose a difficult path. When a river cannot flow due to obstacles in its way, it will find another way to flow, as did my father.

It was during his last battle that his family, and those close to him, saw the tremendous courage of this great warrior.

Chapter 10

The Warrior's Last Battle

When I found out as an adult that Dad had lung cancer and would live only a short time, I regressed to my childhood hole (the hiding place under the stairs). Why did he have to get cancer? How could I live without him? What would Mom do? She has always been so dependent on him. And why, when just three years earlier my brother Gil had died of cancer? I'm sure that was a contributing factor in my father's illness. Worse yet, now that we know what the decaying process of the disease is like, how could we possibly go through it again with Dad? I cried, "Oh God No. Not my Father!"

From my diary:

Sunday, January 16, 1985
The doctors told my Dad that he has six months to live, and now they say he has six weeks. I met this woman for Thanksgiving, and she tells me her father is dying of cancer. It's now December when they tell Dad the same thing. But didn't I know this long ago from a dream? Yeah, I did. My youngest daughter is taking it very hard. She got real sick Monday night on my birthday. I get very scared for her. She is so close to her Grandpa. I look to my children, and their strength helps me, but this, Dad's illness, has really affected her. She says she does not

feel strong. She's taking it too hard. We all are! I feel like I'm falling. Why? Before I got pregnant with my daughter I felt like I was going to fall apart. I feel so bad about Dad and about my hija being so sick over it. But she's a chip off the old block.

February 4, 1985

My eldest daughter said the other night after visiting with Grandpa and Grandma, "Oh Mom, he's such a delight! And he is. I go over to cheer him up and he cheers us up."

Yes, his zest for life is incredible; he now values every minute he's alive. I guess the feeling is contagious because I too value every moment of life. Every day as I wake, I'm thankful for another day of having him in my life. I get sad. I have been waking up at 3:00 in the morning.

I recall a dream I had: Dad and I were outside of the Earth. I remember the words hindsight, insight, and foresight. Father Pat Valdez was in the dream. Are we three from another place or planet, trying to survive in this cold world? I don't know. I know we're different.

What would my life be like without Dad? Okay, I'd wake up in the morning, and he would no longer come to my door. We would not discuss the little things about the system, the family. I would no longer give him food of mine that he loves so much.

I went on after my brother Gil left us, but how did I go on, so neurotically trying to replace or find my brother in others? And then Gil returned to die. I had to let go. But why do the people I love so deeply die of cancer? First Gil, then my best friend, Marcela, now Dad. I think Gil was lonely for our family when he left us. Dad and him had a falling out and Gil stayed away for a long time. Marcela was different and unusually unselfish. Dad was never a part of the system. The only place I've ever fit in is in my own family and friends, and in education. I fit in a halfway house counseling clients, at the University of Colorado and Metropolitan State College teaching, and helping these at risk kids at North High School.

Dad is waiting for all his grandchildren to come to him. Mary Lou, what do you know? Right now, only that I am afraid. What are you afraid of? Get in touch with your own feelings surrounding your own death. Okay. We all have to go through it. Talk about it. When I have a lot of stress, it all goes to my back and neck. And it is stress.

Not cancer! Good! That's my fear, then. Let it go!

March 5, 1986

In my diary during Dad's last days I wrote: "I am tired, very tired. I feel myself clamming up, I have a shell around me. I'm back in the hole, my childhood hiding place. But it's a soft cotton ball. My shell could come down whenever anyone wants to help me. On Monday I followed the ambulance to the hospital. He is so sick. Next Monday they will take more tests on him. I don't know what the hell for!"

My sister, Orlanda, wrote this poem to Dad a month before he died.

"February 10, 1986"

My Birthday Message to My Dad
My heart is heavy—tears overflow.
Your latest struggle has put a damper on your glow.
Suffering and helplessness clouded over in your eyes, a mere reflection of a man so powerful and wise.

Your physical body so frail toward the end—
But those eyes hold a history, so rich my friend.
That really ought to be told around every bend.
A magnificent legacy you leave me, my Dad!
Of a man who wasn't afraid to love his fellow man.

Born ahead of his time, your destiny called you
a Warrior, who would march to the beat of a different
drum and your fire eagerly responded.

With energy, anger and spirit your strong voice resounded,
struggle against injustice—raise hell against war—fight for
the needy—the hungry—the poor, have compassion for tormented souls.

"LOS CAPITALISTAS SE VAN A FREGAR" (The Capitalists are going to be screwed)
Messages recorded,
Messages received, energies passed down—ideas fermented.

Alternatives were many, but your values never wavered.
Your belief in Socialism dominated your soul.
There were times I doubted, didn't really understand—
would you ever realize your goal?

I'm older and wiser now you see—my birthday's today and
I'm past twenty-three, but Daddy to me you'll always be,
One Hell of A Fighter, A Powerful Man, who gave me the
greatest gift of all—a concern for humanity.
From my strongest role model—who even in his frail state
could walk so tall!
An inheritance I'll treasure as I blaze many trails—No way
in hell will I ever fail—to continue the struggle you fought
with conviction.

BLESS YOU DADDY, my greatest benefactor, may you find
PEACE and with your eternal flame, guide me forever—after.
Orlanda Tafoya

My beloved father passed away in his home on March 8,
1986, at the age of 82. His family was all around him. Just before
he died, Mom touched his face and said, "I love you, Roberto, I
love you with all my heart." Tears came rolling down his face
as he listened to his beloved wife, Edna. He said nothing. He
may be gone, but his spirit, beliefs, and commitment to a better world will continue on.

Pat Schroeder related to him with respect and always responded to him. In a condolence letter to the Trujillo family, she wrote:

"I extend my condolences to all of you over the death of Bob. He was one who stood solidly in the world with a vision of justice for all. May each of you find comfort and strength among all your family and friends.

Sincerely,
Pat Schroeder
Congresswoman"

Tom Gavin, staff writer, for *The Denver Post.* March 15, 1986 wrote:

Post-mortem

"He's gone.

The old warrior will battle no more.

Robert Trujillo, Colorado's Chief Communist, has departed this life.

You reacted, didn't you? The word "Communist" had an effect, didn't it? It always does. We are a nation of political nerve-enders, creatures of the conditioned response. Tap the knee and watch the leg fly up. It doesn't take much.

Life would have been much easier for Robert Trujillo if he'd joined the Vegetarian Party back in the '30s and easier for his family, too. In America the path of the Communist is stony.

But I told you, Robert Trujillo was a man of conviction. Deep in the coils of the Great Depression, the Communist Party looked good to the sheepherder/farm worker/coal miner from the San Luis Valley who'd lost two brothers to malnutrition and who was trying to feed a large family in a crippled economy.

He became a Communist and he remained one. Robert Trujillo was no political butterfly and bulldog stubborn.

He paid a price. Repeatedly. But in and out of work and in and out of jail he remained a Marxist.

And community gadfly.

And social conscience.

But Robert Trujillo was different from any political zealot I've ever seen. He was amiable, not grim about it. Called himself "the happy Communist."

It seemed to be so.

He was often in sight, working the edges of crowds, hawking party publications, during the '50s and '60s, and when "The Denver 14"—an assortment of social activists-invaded the state Senate in 1969 to protest inaction on a number of social welfare bills, there was 65-year-old Robert Trujillo in the thick of it.

Changes

"When I was a child," a daughter recalled, "I often thought, 'God, I really don't like being related to this person, he's causing me so much trouble.' 'But later, when I realized what a man of conviction he was, I became very proud."

That pride peaked, Orlanda Tafoya said, when her father was one of the Denver 14. She told him of those deep feelings in a poem written for him. He was far gone in cancer's wasting process then, and tears streamed down his face as he listened.

"Please, he said, read it at my funeral."

She did. In Our Lady of Guadalupe Church last Tuesday.

"It was very, very warm, an almost joyous occasion," Mrs. Tafoya said, "The church was just packed."

You're surprised they'd say goodbye to an old Communist in a church? Don't be. Jose Lara, a fair-to-middling social activist himself, was pastor at Our Lady for 11 years, and Robert Trujillo was there, he recalled, every Sunday.

"Not inside, but outside. Distributing the paper. I don't know what it was called—'The Worker,' I think. He'd put it on the windshields of all the cars."

Eulogy

The former priest [Jose Lara] spoke at the memorial service, recalling Trujillo's San Luis Valley origins "and how rough his life was, of how one of his children died, of how two brothers of nearly the same age died of malnutrition, of how he was a survivor, a strong person. I spoke of his many employments... of his efforts for social justice, and of how it got him arrested in Trinidad and Walsenburg and Denver.

He was a man of strength and passion. I spoke of that. And how he would speak out in any situation.

"And how he was active."

"This is the legacy for his family and friends."

Did Robert Trujillo have an impact?

Not if Colorado Communist Party membership is the measure. "I wouldn't be honest with you if I said yes," Trujillo, then 81, said last summer when asked if it amounted to much. His children link his struggles through the years with things now taken for granted, things like Social Security and pension and welfare benefits.

"Those things didn't just happen," a daughter said. My father always told me, "Somebody builds the fire so that other people can be warmed."

Did Robert Trujillo help bring social reform to America? Perhaps. Who can say?

He didn't bring political tolerance to Colorado, though. Probably you noticed the daughter quoted just above was not identified. She's afraid of economic retaliation, that her husband will be fired if her relationship to the chairman of the Colorado Communist Party is known.

It's not all that odd. It happened many times to Robert Trujillo.

In Colorado a loving daughter cannot publicly embrace her father.

That's very sad." Gavin, "Post-mortem," *The Denver Post*, March, 15 1986.

I Mary Lou Salazar am the daughter that Gavin was referring to, and now, in this book. I publicly embrace my beloved father Robert Trujillo. If my name had come out in this article that my father was a communist, my husband would have probably lost his job. And also I didn't want my children to be exposed to the harassment that my siblings and I went through.

One of the greatest joys in my life was the beautiful friendship my father and I shared. I felt like something inside me had died after my father passed away. I felt that when he left, there would never be any more love, at least not his kind of genuine love. Even though I had my own beautiful, loving family, life for a time seemed meaningless. I felt that nobody besides my husband ever loved me quite as much as my father did.

The grief has lifted; the missing him has not. He was at my home almost every day, to just read the newspaper, to talk, to listen, to walk his dog, to see his grandchildren, to lecture and discuss politics, current events, and personal problems.

The mentor of my life is not at my door anymore, but he is in my heart, in my life, in my thoughts every single day, and he'll never go away. I will tell the true meaning of life from what he taught me: Love, pure love, is what moves one to action.

April 18, 1986

Today is April 18, a month and ten days after Dad died. Easter was very hard. We all went to the mountains to spread Dad's ashes. Virgil and I will take some of his ashes to drop around the Stations of the Cross in the San Luis Valley.

Even in the aftermath of his life, Dad's legacy continues on in many different ways, especially here in Colorado.

The Aftermath

Months after you have passed on, tears roll down my face, the agony of the human race. North's the scapegoat for Reagan's lies; I still see apathy in people's eyes.

The loneliness I feel for you,
the current of love,
the volcano in me has yet to rise,
the passion, the love inside my eyes.
I miss you, Dad, but you know I know we never die, you know I still cry, you know I will carry on, you know the man who spent so many hours with me knew what he was doing, how you were grooming me.

Like the tide I will rise again, the pent-up emotions out of me will blend in perfect harmony. The anger, the love, the fear will all explode, but I'll do it my way, through my children, my teaching, my political activity, my patience, and my faith. One hundred percent of me will be, one hundred percent of what you left me.

Mary Lou Salazar

Magdalena Gallegos, freelance writer, wrote:

A People's History of Colorado

There was some controversy about who was to be chosen for the mural. Of course, Robert Trujillo was one of the controversial ones. He was a communist. It all started in December of 1989 when Richard Castro, the Director of Community Relations for the city of Denver, wrote an article entitled, "80's Decade Dedication Won't Apply To The 90's" in *La Voz*, in which he mentioned some of the Chicano civil rights leaders.

Trujillo's grandson read the article and approached his mother (Mary Lou Salazar) with, "Mom, they left Grandpa out of the article." Mom (Mary Lou Salazar) wrote a letter to the paper that had printed Castro's letter:

> "To leave Robert Trujillo out of the article was like leaving the Native Americans out of American History." She continued, "Robert Trujillo was well known to the Denver community for his leadership as the chairman of the Colorado Communist Party who spent his entire life working to improve conditions for the oppressed."

Richard Castro, Executive Director of the Agency for Human Rights and Community Relations, wrote to me after I had written the article to *La Voz* about his article excluding my father. Richard wrote:

February 6, 1990

"Dear Mary Lou:
I am writing this letter to you regarding your article that appeared in the January 24, 1990 issue of *La Voz*. I want to assure you that I did not intend to leave out your father in my previous article. As you know, I had the utmost respect and admiration for him. I was honored that I had an opportunity to visit with him before he passed away.

I am glad that you took the time to highlight his career in your article. He was indeed one of our leaders and mentors during the difficult period of the 50's up through the 80's."

Sincerely,"
Richard Castro
Executive Director

Magdalena Gallegos continued:

"Soon after Salazar wrote the letter to *La Voz* in which the article appeared, she received a call from a woman who had read her letter in *La Voz* and who said she cried when she read about Roberto Trujillo's life. She asked for and got Mary Lou Salazar's phone number. And she called Salazar at her home. She advised Salazar to contact Barbara Revelle, who was working on a Colorado History Mural for the Convention Center. Salazar went to Barbara Revelle and took piles of material about Robert Trujillo. Mary Lou Salazar persuaded Barbara Revelle to include her father in the mural."

In August, 1991 our family had a celebration honoring our father's mural on the Denver Convention Center in downtown Denver, Colorado. The following story was published in 1991 by Magdalena Gallegos in *Urban Spectrum:*

The Other Side Of History: Robert Trujillo, The Happy Communist

He was a Communist!

"This was a fact he offered no apologies for. He was a champion of the little guy—of the workers, and he fought for them and he worked for them all of his life. He was as close to a hero as anyone I've ever known."

These were Ricardo La Fore's words as he paid tribute to the late Roberto Trujillo at a celebration in honor of the man's inclusion in "A People's History of Colorado" mural at the Denver Convention Center.

Trujillo's family recently invited friends and family to help celebrate the historic event. They met at the downtown Convention Center to view the mural, then caravaned to the Sheraton Graystone Castle for an afternoon of music, singing, dining and sharing remembrances of the incredible life of Roberto Trujillo.

Ricardo La Fore (a community activist) recalled his first encounter with Trujillo. "There was a Communist meeting going on at Our Lady of Guadalupe Church Hall. I couldn't believe what I was hearing. 'My God,' I thought. 'This man (Trujillo) is really talking the party line. This is the real thing.' I grew up in the early days of the Chicano Movement and you hadn't even cut your teeth unless someone had called you a Communist. I worked for the United Farm Workers and everyone called us Communists even though we were not. So when I met Mr. Trujillo, who really was a Communist, I said, 'Far out.'

"Trujillo was funny, too," Ricardo La Fore said. "I remember a young lady who was running for political office in North Denver. Her campaign promise was to run the hookers out of North Denver. She went to Mr. Trujillo's house to tell him what she was going to do if elected. He said, 'Wait a minute. Let me see if I understand this correctly. There are murderers, thieves and drug dealers and the world is going to hell and you are promising to get the hookers out of North Denver? At least they're working!'

Trujillo wasn't your everyday, ordinary Communist. He made an impression on people from all walks of life, including some Catholic priests and nuns. A priest from Our Lady of Guadalupe Catholic Church once joked that Trujillo was one of his best parishioners. He never missed a Sunday Mass. He always was outside handing out fliers and leafleting all the cars."

Craig Hart, a former priest arrested with the Denver 14 in 1969, was one of the priests who knew Trujillo in the 60s and he spoke at the mural celebration. Hart said:

I met Roberto in a parking lot with a bunch of fliers under his arm. He was putting fliers on all the cars in the lot. I'll bet he's up in heaven still handing out fliers. The next time I saw Roberto, he told me about the Massacre at Ludlow. After that I tagged around him trying to learn more about the histories and accomplishments he had been involved with. [See the Massacre at Ludlow in the Appendix, page 161.]

I remember the time we set up tents in front of the Immaculate Conception Cathedral and Bob [Robert] brought his cot down and slept with us. We were trying to get some farm worker legislation passed.

The next morning we gathered on the steps of the Cathedral and decided to go to the Senate for a confrontation. Bob asked if we minded if he went with us. Everyone agreed he should go.

Fourteen of us went and took over the Senate: Two nuns, five priests and Robert Trujilllo, head of the Communist Party of Colorado, made the front page of the news the next day.

The Archbishop called us in to see him and he was more than slightly upset. He said he knew it was becoming fashionable for priests and nuns to get arrested but did we have to be hanging around a Communist?

Craig Hart at a later date wrote:

Why did the life of Jesus spring into my mind when Mary Lou asked me if I would like to share some of my impressions in her book about her lovely and inspiring father, Bob? Of course, I immediately recalled Jesus' discourse on the arrival of a revolutionary new order-new at least in the eyes of his contemporaries, and most especially of the ruling order of his time, the institutional spiritually of Israel and the Roman Empire. The Eight Beatitudes were to be the "Constitution" of the new order. " Happy those who hunger and thirst for what is right: they shall be satisfied. Happy the peacemakers: they shall be called brothers and sisters of God. Happy those who are persecuted in the cause of right: theirs is the kingdom of heaven." We have in another place of the Christian New Testament, the account of Jesus's supposed best friends, who dispersed after his murder and burial. Three days later they are on the run, hiding out and having dinner with a stranger at Emmaus. It was only after eating together-sharing a meal-that their eyes (their minds) opened and recognized it was their friend who was supposed to be dead. Their awareness wasn't limited to just the recognition of the man with whom they had spent the last three years. More importantly, they started to figure out what he was talking about all the time. "Oh yeah, this is what the new order means. This is what Jesus was/is. This is what it means to be a human being. This is what we mean to each other. This is what it means to..."

This new understanding was passed on by word
of mouth for 50–60 years before taking on the form
of the written gospels. All that was written was, in
fact, the result and benefit of what 'til this day is
not 20/20 hindsight. Reflection, discussion, arguing over and attempting to live out the what Jesus
(and others like him, including Bob Trujillo was saying only laid the foundation. So that all of us can
in fact come to that. "Oh yeah, I see who you are, I
understand all humans, all of life for what it is. I see
what you meant when you said..." Oh yeah, I see
what you meant and therefore who you really are
and what you embodied with your life when we sit
down, talk and eat a shared (our lives) meal... There
is after all enough to go around—don't be afraid,
there is enough to go around—trust.

Even thought it's been but a twinkling of a few
years since Bob's going to heaven, we knew then
and know now that he had a burning hunger and
unquenchable thirst for justice. He was the consum-
mate peacemaker. In giving ourselves the opportunity to reflect, discuss, critique and even argue on
him and the history we are now creating, we reap
the benefit of a still-to-be-clarified hindsight of his
too few years among us. And like men and women
of all generations, we too are saying "Oh yeah, this
is what you meant, Bob. This is who you were. Oh I
get it Bob, this is what all of those days in jail meant,
for you; all of those flyers you had printed for us
to read and reflect on; all of those picket lines you
walked burning with the hope that soon, real soon
the new order would become reality." Bob, with
each new moment, day, year and lifetime of hindsight, I'm seeing that our lives, spent in giving them
away truly are the grist by which we come to recognize who and what we mean to each other.

What continues to be your life's message that I'm
starting to feel and at last recognize? Didn't you say,
like Buddha, like Jesus, like King, like Chavez, **the**

new order is due. Long overdue! That it is time for us to bring an end to "better." Instead, "We are all One," or in your words, "We are in communion, We are all One, We are communists." And an end to "better". I see now that what you were saying is that "better" is indeed one of the most seductive ideas, an opiate, ever visited upon the human race. The idea that for anyone, any color, any gender, any religion, any nation is somehow superior to another only sucks us into wanting more of what we imagine we need to be happy (happy are those...). And didn't you gently tell all of us that we operate from the false thought that there is not enough of the things we need in order to have a happy life on this planet. And as long as we hold in our minds that there is not enough stuff we need, we're going to be in competition for it (for more). But worse yet, in our country, we've decided before the competition begins, who the winners are going to be.

Corporate capitalism and its latest development, globalization, are saying, "Oh by the way, if you are Black and I'm White, if you are male and I'm a female, if you're Third World, if you're the air we breathe and the water we drink, I'm going to win before we start." History always has someone saying we're "better" out of the root thought there is insufficient stuff to go around-not enough food, not enough God. Your message, your life said, "My way in not better." But "there are simply other ways while we're in the business of living, simply share. There's enough to go around. We are all one, we're all communist."

Each day from sixth grade through eighth grade of my Catholic school, on the upper-right-hand corner of our classroom green board, nuns wrote, *"Pray for the conversion of Russia."* Hindsight once again suggests that at that time I was praying for the conversion of all Communists, including Bob Trujillo who was either in jail, printing flyers, walking a

picket line for worker's medical benefits or latrines
in the fields for farm workers or working damned
hard to bring another day of living for his family and
friends. God help all of us if those prayers worked.
Bob didn't need conversion. Bob already knew that
"E Pluribus Unum" meant not just a "One from
Many" for Americans—but "One Family of Humankind from the great Diversity of Humankind." Bob
knew in his bones, he was born with the core belief,
that not only Americans should "Trust in God" but
that Humankind should "Trust in God."

Tonight, I'll pray to Bob, Edna, Frankie, all of his
family and all brothers and sisters who are communicating with us for the Kingdom of justice, peace
and plenty to carry high the Fire of Love, Justice and
Oneness burning and thirsting inside of all of us.

Even in death, controversy follows Trujillo. A guest speaker
at the celebration was Barbara Jo Revelle, the creator of the
mural. She said:

Mr. Trujillo led a difficult life, a life of struggle and
pain. He grew up in the Depression. Lost two brothers to malnutrition and lost a son and grandson.
He was a sheepherder and a coal miner, but he was
never defeated by all that. He wasn't a quitter. He
was a survivor.

And probably those times gave him the power,
the spirit, and the anger to stand up for what he
believed in. We can call what he believed in by many
different names and some of those names make people nervous-and one of those names is Communist!

There were also controversies surrounding the
Ludlow Massacre and the Massacre at Sand Creek.
There are people in the mural from both sides.
Again some questioned, "Why do we have to represent these things. We're not proud of these incidents of racism and hatred." Revelle says the mural
is not a whitewash. It's very important to represent

those struggles and to show that everything wasn't always terrific and nice here. A lot of people had to pay the price with their lives and sometimes for the work they did.[21]

Abelardo (Lalo) Delgado came to the United States from Mexico in 1943. He was a novelist and poet who taught citizenship classes at Metropolitan State College. He read the poems he had written about Dad at the mural celebration in August, 1991.

CAMARADA, PART I

El buen caudillo, (The good chief or leader)
Robert Trujillo,
stays controversial
long after his death.
On a mural wall
his face among great
Hispanic leaders
deserves attention.
Known for his good deeds,
his strong advocacy
for those defenseless,
was his life time task.
His political

                              Ideology

Belies his Christian
way of responding
to the basic needs

                     of his fellow man

and fellow woman.
Many a struggle,
many a just cause

---

[21] Gallegos, "The Other Side Of History: Roberto Trujillo, The Happy Communist," *The Urban Spectrum*, November, 1991. Volume 5, Number 8, November, 1991.

are now but the ghosts
joining his picture
calling passers-by
to keep the guard up.
Some guerrilleros (participant in warfare)
just as valientes (brave)
as he join in praise,
in acknowledgement
of prints his life made.
The most heroic

deeds are not always

bloody battlefiends
but the waking up
each morning to raise
the poor man's banner,
to advocate hard
day after day

for those whose extreme

suffering renders
them tongue tied. To speak
with new eloquence
of due social change.

CAMARADA,

PART 2

We've come to contemplate
his face among the great
in this mosaico wall
decorating with pride
our convention center.
There's no doubt you belong
in this selected group.
Future school children will come
to visit, perhaps ask,
_What did he do, teacher? _
_Dedicated his life
to the plight of workers. _
Knowing teachers will answer.
There're acts of heroism

worth purple hearts, medals
of honor in the streets
of Denver U.S.A.
and Robert Trujillo
has earned a few of them.
We see him and we say,
—Muchas gracias, yea, thanks,
        thanks for being a source
        of mucho orgullo, (a lot of pride)
        not just for Chicanos
        but for all who also
        share a sense of justice.—
In our communities
tenemos de todo, (we have everybody)
farm workers, confused teens
who think gangs are so cool
and killing each other
a way to show manhood,
we have tecatos, (tecate beer drinkers)
winos, welfare mothers,
hardworking and honest
people who go to church,
we have talented artists, even city mayors,
professors, movie stars,
singers and scientists,

so why not include him
whose climb to fame includes
being a good parent,
a good camarada,
alma colorada. (red soul)

*Robert's four sisters: From left, Odelia, Della,
Madeline, and Frances.*

Edna and Robert.

Orlanda (baby) and Edna.

Orlanda behind Robert, Mary Lou (baby) on
Robert's lap, Rena at the right.

*Edna, Orlanda at the right, Mary Lou (baby) on
Edna's lap and Rena to the left.*

Gil on pony.

Edna far left, Gil, Orlanda standing Rena,
Ruth, and Mary Lou.

Jessica and her great grandma and grandpa
Trujillo and Yo Yo.

Mothers For Peace

The day after the mural celebration, I traveled to the United Kingdom. Because of my work for peace, I was chosen by the Mothers for Peace organization in Colorado as a delegate to meet and join with women from different countries to visit England and the Mothers for Peace organization in England. I spent two weeks sharing experiences and values with women from around the world. It was heartwarming to join women from different countries who believe in and work for peace in our world. I am most grateful for my wonderful parents, who passed on their value of peace. I am proud to be another Mother for Peace.

What follows is a poem I read about Mom. Behind, or rather alongside, every strong man is a strong woman, and this was the case with my mother.

"My Mom"
A lot of poems have been written, a lot of songs have been sung, but none of them can describe our mom.
A woman timid, a woman shy, she was afraid to go out in the world and fly. She never worked outside our home, with nine children to roam she never felt alone.
She gave us a life that was good, although sometimes we misunderstood; she always tried to understand and gave us her helping hand. She was often sick and she was weak, but now we know that she was strong with feelings deep. She helped us grow, she helped us be. She is our mother, she is our love, and she's the sun that shines from heaven above.

Mary' Lou Salazar

Our Mother Joins our Father

June 10, 1990

My beloved mother passed away four years after my father died. She died June 10, 1990, with all her children and extended family around her. In the last moments of her life, my son, who had flown in with his wife, whispered in Mom's ear, "Grandma, remember when I was little I sat on your lap and you sang this song to me? 'Yo ti amo Dios mio de me corazon. Detesto mes culpas, te pido perdon. Perdon, perdon, Dios mio perdon.* *(I love you, my God of my heart. I detest my faults, I ask for your pardon, pardon, pardon, my God pardon).' The whole family surrounding her bed held hands and joined in singing. My beautiful mother lifted her head up, and tears rolled down her face. When my son was done leading the song, Mom gently dropped her head and passed to spirit.

Actually, I felt I had lost my mother when my father passed away. She loved him more than life. She was so depressed after he died that she seemed to have lost her will to live. She hung in there for four years after he died, but the love of her life was gone, and her zest for life went with him.

My father's spirit lives on, as does all that he believed in and practiced. He spent the better part of his life working towards building a just world.

His Spirit Lives On

A few moments before my father passed away, he whispered to me, "Mary Lou, you teach Marxism!" He repeated it two more times. With tears rolling down my face, I answered, "I will Dad, I will."

In light of that last talk with my father, I here write a brief section on the theory of Marxism.

Marxism

Marxism is a theory of the world and of human society as a part of that world. Marxism takes its name from Karl Marx (1818–1883), who, together with Frederick Engels (1820–1895), created the theory during the middle and latter part of the 1800's. Marx and Engels embarked on discovering why human society is the way it is, why it changes, and what further changes are in store for humankind. Their inquiry led them to the conclusion that these changes, like the changes in external nature, are not accidental, but follow certain laws. This shared view made it possible for them to work out a scientific theory of society that is based on the actual experience of people, as opposed to vague notions about society, notions associated with religious beliefs, race and hero-worship, personal inclinations, or utopian dreams.

Marx's early work focused on alienation, as in his *Economic and Philosophical Manuscript* of 1844. His later economic critique of capitalism and visions of socialism and communism were intended to establish a system that would create an unalienated human being. He felt that modern capitalist society, like other pre-socialist forms, produced the alienated human being. He studied the modes of production and argued that when men and women are connected with their work, as in primitive communal/communist society, they do not experience the alienation that many experience under capitalism.

The basic thought running through Marx's theory is that economic ownership and production and the structure of society of every historical epoch necessarily arising there-from constitute the foundation for the political and intellectual history of that epoch; that consequently, ever since the dissolution of the primeval communal ownership of land, all history has been a history of class struggles, of struggles between exploited and dominating classes at various stages of social development; but that this struggle had now reached a stage in which the exploited and oppressed class (the proletariat) can no longer emancipate itself from the class that exploits and oppresses it (the bourgeoisie) without at the same time forever freeing the whole of society from exploitation, oppression, and class struggles.

I put this chart together to illustrate Marx's theory of the stages of development. As each stage has advanced toward modern market society, people have become more and more alienated.

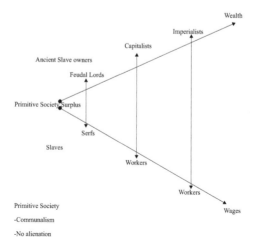

Primitive Society

-Communalism
-No alienation
-Relations of production essentially collective
-The main divisions of labor were by sex and age
-No classes of exploiters and exploited
-Lands were held in common, and tools and utensils were owned directly by those who used them
-Products of the land were for use, not for sale

Feudal Society

-The emergence of commodity production, economically based classes, and the coercive state emerged.
-Improvements in agricultural techniques laid the basis for economic inequalities.
-Workers experienced alienation from the products and process of their labor, from competition with others workers, and ultimately from themselves.
-Workers became a commodity, whose human value was equated with their market value.

Capitalist Society

-Private ownership of the means of production became increasingly concentrated.
-Owners and workers became freed of the arbitrary fetters of feudalism, but workers became increasingly alienated.
-Society became increasingly divided into two classes of exploiters and exploited.
-Production became increasingly efficient, creating vastly greater wealth than in previous systems.

Imperialism

-Globalization of capitalist exploitation as owners sought cheap raw materials, cheap labor, and expanded markets.
-Increased competition among capitalist nations, leading to wars.

Imperialism extended the power and dominion of a nation, actually of its dominant class, either by direct territorial acquisition or by indirect control over the political or economic life of other areas, lands and peoples.

This extension of power typically overrode the will of the people. In effect, imperialism has come to comprise a global monopoly of the owning class. [22]

An actual socialist society, like all previous forms of society, would come into existence only on the basis of what had existed before it. The contradictions of earlier social forms would transform them into more advanced and protective forms. According to Marx, the most advanced economic system prior to socialism was capitalism. He did not design the new socialist or communist visions in any great detail, but he did identify their main features. Under socialism, all productive property would be collectively owned, and people would be paid according to their work. Finally, with the "withering away of the coercive state," full communism would arrive with a democratically and cooperatively managed economy based on justice conceived as "To each according to need, from each according to ability."

For Marx socialism and communism represent the first emergence, the genuine actualization of man's nature as fully realized, with alienation overcome. In Marx's words: "The whole concept of man, his real needs, are rooted in his nature; this distinction between real and false needs is possible only on the basis of a picture of the nature of man and the true needs rooted in his nature. Man's true needs are those whose fulfillment is necessary for the realization of his essence as a human being." To sum up: "The existence of what I truly love is felt by me as a necessity, as a need, without which my essence cannot be fulfilled, satisfied, complete."[23]

---

[22]   See Lenin's *Imperialism: The Highest Stage of Capitalism.*
       International Publishers, New York

[23]   Erich Fromm. *Marx's Concept of Man*. New York: (Frederick Ungar Publishing Company, 1961.) page 62-MEGA I, 1 a, pl84.

A communist economy would serve the needs of the people, not the profits of owners. High priorities would include free health care, free education, and jobs for everyone who is able to work. To avoid invasion by capitalist powers, communism anywhere would require communism everywhere.

My father once told me that if socialism did not prove to work for the good of the people, the people must then build a better system and work towards bringing that new order into existence. Most of the modern socialist systems have now gone capitalist.

What I think in large part went wrong—and I believe my father would agree, is that years of conditioning of greed and power are ingrained into the minds of people under the capitalist system. People are not going to transform into caring about one another just because a new social order takes over. [In C.W. Mills. The Power Elite] C. Wright Mills shows that the people in the lowest class still are conditioned with the values of the elite. The contradictions that came out of the previous stages of development have now created economic globalization and an international monopoly of power and greed forcing the crisis around the world today. With unemployment, continual wars, poverty, and injustices, perhaps the people will bring about something better in the way of a more decent and democratic world society. In addition I feel that the new order must incorporate spirituality, individuality, creativity, and critically thinking and universal preventive methods to protect the environment for the survival of the planet among the citizens of the world.

Dad's spirit lives on in newspapers and in the hearts of his family members. The following are 1991 excerpts of columnist Tomas Romero of The Denver Post regarding family and friends honoring my father.

Family and friends of Robert and Edna Trujillo gathered on Sunday to observe the "honoring of El Senor Trujillo," whose image now graces the new Convention Center wall mural. Trujillo is in fine company. Section number 7 also holds for public esteem Min Yasui, Corky Gonzales, Sam Sandos, George

Sandoval, Ricardo Falcon, Tim Watson, Lowell Thomas, Damon Runyon and others.

Even in a group of notables, Robert Trujillo stands out from the rest. He was a communist.

Trujillo, who died in 1986 at age 82, was a life-long communist, Mexican American, and American who advocated the peaceful overthrow of the government, which he believed failed to provide justice for people. I never met Trujillo; yet, I am certain I would have crossed the street to avoid confronting him-that was then and that was me then. Those who knew him—his familia— and friends such as Father Craig Hart and Ricardo LaFore, who were exposed to both his passion and pain, were blessed.

The following excerpts are from my firstborn daughter's words about her grandpa Trujillo in 1993:

I feel so good. Love is coming. I feel positive vibes. I'm traveling on the right path. Grandpa's watching me from Heaven.

I am five years old, a curious wanderer searching, for the meaning of everything in life.

Why Grandpa, do we plant a garden?

Grandpa says, "To grow food my hija, to understand why and how life exists. Watching a garden grow teaches us of how we need to grow, and how we must take care of ourselves."

"But why do we need to know that. Grandpa?" I ask.

Grandpa replies, "To understand that we as humans are only a small part of a much larger life force. What's a life force? Grandpa, did the garden stop growing when you died?"

Grandpa's words come into my mind. "The garden never stopped growing. It's in your mind, another part of our existence. I'm with you helping you grow, my Hija."

I smile deep inside where time has no limits. Where I feel a warm glow. I know the garden is love in my life and that I must cultivate it always and forever.

Grandpa, guide me through to a positive place.

Help me face what I have to face. Help me to always grow like the garden grows!

Love you!

My father always planted a garden with vegetables, and he taught my children to appreciate the food chain of life.

The following words of Fidel Castro fit nicely with my daughter's story: "We insist once again on what we said on other occasions: if you want the child to care for the garden, teach him to plant the garden and no one will have to lecture him on caring for it, no one will have to keep behind him with a stick to keep him from destroying the garden; teach him to plant a tree, and no one will have to punish him for destroying trees. Those who do not create, destroy. Those who haven't the least experience in what creation is, destroy."[24]

On September 22, 1991, Dad's granddaughter, my youngest daughter, wrote:

Grandpa, I love you so very much, and I miss you. I still remember everything that you talked to me about. I still live by your words of love and wisdom.

I never got to tell you face to face what a great man you are, like the things you used to do to help all people was great.

I don't think I'm mad at you for leaving me, but why did you have to leave me so soon? I had so many things that I wanted to learn from you. I

---

[24]   *Education In Revolution* 1975 La Habana: Instituto Cubano Del Libro 1975. P. 6.

needed you to show me so much more than you did. And now who will teach me or show me all that I need to learn? There isn't anyone who knows what you know about how to love and forgive and to always fight for justice. I just keep remembering the times we had together before you died in your room, when you would only eat with me. And you were playing with me making me laugh when you were in so much pain. Why would you only eat with me? Was it that you loved me that much?

Remember the time when I was four, and I went with you and Michael to your house, and my mom didn't know you took us. And we played upstairs, and you laid on your lawn chair out back. Then my mom came over "going crazy" looking for us. She got so mad at both you and me for not telling her we were going with you. We had a lot of fun times together, huh? Like all the times I would mess up your hair while you were trying to talk to my mom and dad and you would get mad at me. But I knew you weren't mad.

My youngest daughter gives credit to her grandfather for her strong values. She recently wrote in a school newspaper, "I have two wonderful parents, an older sister and an older brother. I have been deeply influenced by my Grandfather, Robert Trujillo, because of his love, strength, fairness, and his firm belief in justice."

Jessica is Dad's great granddaughter and my granddaughter. She shared some memories of her great grandpa with me.

When I was four years old, I remember I wanted my grandpa Trujillo to give me some money for an ice cream at the store down the corner. I went up to him, kissed him, and said, "Grandpa, give me some money!" I was all excited and I remember my mom yelled at me and said "No! Don't do that." And grandpa told my mom, "Let me take care of her." He put me on his lap and said, "My Jessica, when I was a young boy, I worked all the time and barely made a dollar for a full day's work. You have to learn that things in life are not handed to you; you need to earn them." I was four and all I knew was I wanted that money to buy my ice cream. Grandpa then took me to the garden and showed me how to pull up the weeds, "Not the flowers," he said that over and over to make sure I didn't pick the flowers. I did it and he gave me fifty cents. I knew that wasn't a lot, and I said I wanted more money. Grandpa then took me inside and had me help Grandma Trujillo. He told her to make me do something, so she put me on a chair to help her with the dishes, only a few cups, but it seemed like the biggest pile in the world to me! Grandpa told her to not just give money to me. He was teaching me a lesson, and if she just gave me money, I wouldn't understand the value of working for my money. After that day, I always remember the importance of what he taught me. I worked for and earned my dollar and got to buy my ice cream with my own money. He taught me that everyone has to work; nothing is free or handed to me in life, even from my loved ones. I recall my mom watching us, and she knew that grandpa was a great man. She also saw how well I listened to him. I also remember jumping on his big tummy and kissing him. He is always with me, now and forever.

I saw the impact of Dad's life. The people he affected, his work, and his accomplishments were many. Did he create a socialist world? No. But he did by his example create a socialist touch, which helped a lot of the common people in the state of Colorado.

Chapter 12

Conclusion

Dad was a communist, but he was first a man who never accepted injustice. His emotions, his physical being, his spirit, his intellectual power, all combined, were focused in one direction: the path to building socialism. This was his dream: that mankind could love and care, that cooperation would thrive, that lives would be spared, that life could be free from exploitation, hate, and war.

Dad lived a difficult life. He was born into the working class, and the loss of his two baby brothers, the deaths of his father and teenage sister left a lasting impact of pain in him. He carried the sole responsibility of supporting his mother and sisters at the early age of sixteen. When he was twenty-three, he married my mother. Shortly after that the Depression hit, and he lost his job in the coal mine. Mom and Dad had several small children while they were dealing with the many challenges during that period. Dad attended meetings and soon became an organizer and leader who wanted to influence others in the same situation to work towards socialism. In and out of jail all his life, he faced a continual series of crises straggling to gain employment, fight prejudice and racism, and feed his own family.

Dad was driven towards communism during the deep Depression. And his life's path never wavered from the direction of trying to build a just society.

Some gains were accomplished during his lifetime, particularly during the Depression. Because of the pressure of many people around the nation, including the Communist Party leadership and its members, Social Security, pensions, unemployment benefits in America, and jobs for the unemployed came about during this epoch.

People learned about the positive influences of unity, and some activists, including Communist Party leaders and members, continued their efforts after the Depression. They were instrumental in helping lead many just causes, such as forming unions, agitating people during the civil-rights period to create programs that helped all races, bringing an end to the war in Vietnam, and mounting the Poor People's Campaign. It was a time that brought the poor together to demand from the government that their conditions of poverty and injustice be addressed.

The major circumstances and events that influenced Dad's life and built his character, life style, and vocation during the period of 1903 to 1986 were: his home and family environment, his feelings of responsibility surrounding his father's death, the Catholic religion and his Catholic education, the American system, especially the political and economic system, his marriage and children, and his many challenges, particularly his experiences facing racial discrimination before, during, and after the Depression years. All of these factors resulted in his decision to stand up and fight against injustices and racism in America. These major influences helped shape, form, and transform my father.

After Dad died, a memorial service was held at Our Lady of Guadalupe Catholic Church. The church was packed with many family members, friends, and comrades who came to pay their respects to my father.

On Easter Sunday, family and friends scattered his ashes in the Colorado River and around the Stations of the Cross in the San Luis Valley. And I spread some of his ashes on my plants. So parts of him are giving life to flowers, and some will drink him in the water. Others like me who knew him well will receive his spirit of wisdom daily. A man such as he will never die. I now seldom cry. He is so much a part of me.

Robert Trujillo's spirit will never die. Love can never end. Courage never bends. The seed of life has no end; a process continues on. He comes to me in dreams: his strength, his smile, and his love. He was ahead of his time. He was a visionary for a better world. His powers of conviction and love, his goodness, call it what you may, we can see the miracles of his life every day. We cannot see him per se, but we can see the spirit of his love all around us. I see the light of wisdom Dad left me, and I can see, through my relationships with others, the manifestation of his love, of his teachings, and of his goodness in those who knew him well.

Afterthought

My best friend, my father, my relationship with you has no end. I see your face at my door. I cry a little bit less each day because you're not here any more. I cry because I understand you so well. I so knew your anger and your pain. I understand that it has to rain.

I understand your love. Your pain, your anger, it was all the same. Accused of being insane, yet a "humanist" is more your name.

I still miss you, but I'm accepting birth, life, and death and its continuation in the river of life. Feelings stir inside of me, feelings close to a volcano. See, I also understand that you were but a man, striving to be free. At times fear moved you. but a fearful man hides, a courageous man acts. Every action creates a reaction, and at all costs until you passed away, you never gave up your principles and beliefs. For that I salute you. This is what you are still teaching me. In my view it takes a giant of a man to be a communist in a capitalist society. I learned courage from you. I learned never to give up my values and my principles, and I've learned so much more.

Hey, guess what? It's good to cry now that I understand why you had to die. It was time for you to go. Your life's work was done. And now it's our turn to make the river flow.

Round and Round

When I die, go ahead cry.
But guess what?
It's not the end!
Only a continuation
of the ride around again.

The world's not flat,
It's round, my friend.
And we can't fall off
of the end.

We have to come back
around again.

So lets get it right my friend.
We'll all come back.
There's no end.

It's round and round and
round again.

Mary Lou Salazar

The Ludlow Massacre 1913–14

In 1998 Bill Briggs, The Denver Post wrote:

Artifacts of Violence

The crisp nip of autumn had barely kissed the southern Colorado Mountains in 1913 when tempers finally boiled over in the mines.

The hills were alive with some 11,000 men who were carving deeper and deeper into the earth to pull out lumps of coal. Their employer was the Colorado Fuel & Iron Corporation, owned by the vastly rich Rockefeller family.

Wages were low, and working conditions were treacherous in the coal camps. The miners, paid for how much they dug, wanted coal scales checked daily. They demanded to be paid in money instead of scrip. They asked that safety rules be followed, and they pushed for union recognition.

That September, after a union organizer was murdered, the miners walked off the job in protest. Bosses immediately evicted the men and their families from company-owned shacks in the mining towns.

The fight was on.

"When they called the strike, there was this one night when the miners all just came streaming out (of the hills)," says Mark Walker, field director of the Ludlow archaeology dig. "The strike was 40 miles long from Trinidad to Walsenburg. So in all these canyons, people were just pouring out of them."

The United Mine Workers rented nearby plots of land and supplied thousands of tents, setting up about 10 temporary colonies for the striking miners. The men continued picketing while their families made do—cooking in the dirt and playing under the stars.

It got ugly fast.

The Baldwin-Felts Detective Agency hired guns brought in by Rockefeller interests— periodically sprayed the tent colony with bullets. They would drive through the area in an armored car mounted with a machine gun. In the camps, people called it "The Death Special."

Some miners died from the gunfire. Many families dug cellars under their tents to protect women and children from the deadly raids. But the mining companies even invaded the strikers' sleep, training huge spotlights over the tents at night.

The strikers hung on; the mines were unable to operate. Finally, Colorado Governor Elias Ammons dispatched the National Guard. The Rockefellers supplied the soldiers' wages, according to Howard Zinn's book, *A People's History of the United States.*

The miners at first thought the Guard was sent to protect them, and greeted its arrival with flags and cheers. They soon found out the Guard was there to destroy the strike,

Zinn wrote. "Guardsmen beat miners, arrested them by the hundreds....And still the miners refused to give in."

When they lasted through the cold winter of 1913-14, it became clear that extraordinary measures would be needed to break the strike.

By April, 1914, two National Guard companies were positioned in the hills looking down on the largest colony, Ludlow, where about 1,200 people huddled in 200 neatly rowed tents.

On the morning of April 20, the miners and their families were celebrating Greek Easter. By 10 a.m., hundreds of soldiers had ringed the small camp. About then, their commander, Lt. Karl Lindenfelter, signaled his men to open fire. Briggs, "Artifacts Of Violence," *The Denver Post,* August 1998.

The Smith Act.
June 28, 1940, Smith Act
Title 1 of the Act as follows:

Sec. 2(a) It shall be unlawful for any person
1. to knowingly or willfully advocate, abet, advise, or teach the duty, necessity, desirability, or propriety of overthrowing or destroying any government in the United States by force or violence, or by the assassination of any officer of any such government;
2. with the intent to cause the overthrow or destruction of any government in the United States, to print, publish, edit, issue, circulate, sell, distribute or publicly display any written or printed matter advocating, advising, or teaching the duty, necessity, desirability, or propriety of overthrowing or destroying any government in the United States by force or violence;
3. to organize or help to organize any society, group, or assembly of persons who teach, advocate, or encourage the overthrow or destruction of any government in the United States by force or violence, or to be or become a member of, or affiliate with, any such society, group or assembly of persons, knowing the purpose thereof.
(b) For the purposes of this section, the term "government in the United States" means the government of any State, Territory, or possession of the United States, the government of the District of Columbia, or the government of any political subdivision of any of them.

The Supreme Court Case, Trujillo v. City of Walsenburg

10S Colo. 427
Trujillo et al. v. City of Walsenburg
No. 14794.
Supreme Court of Colorado
Nov. 3, 1941

1. Constitutional law ~274

The privilege of a citizen of the United States to use streets and parks for communication of views on national questions is not absolute but relative, and must be exercised in subordination to the general comfort and convenience and in consonance with peace and good order, but it must not, in the guise of regulation, be bridged or denied. U.S.C.A. Amend. 14, ~1.

2. Constitutional law ~ 292

The authority of a municipality to impose regulations in order to assure the safety and convenience of the people in the use of public highways is not inconsistent with civil liberties, but is one of means of guarding the good order upon which they ultimately depend. U.S.C.A. Const. Amend.
118 P.2d—6S/2/2

3. Constitutional law ~292

Where restriction of the use of highways is designed to promote the public convenience in the interest of all, it cannot be disregarded by the attempted exercise of some civil rights, which in other circumstances would be entitled to protection. U.S.C.A. Const. Amend. 14, ~1

4. Constitutional law ~235, 292

An ordinance providing that it shall be unlawful to use streets for any parade, processions, or streets assemblage without first obtaining a permit from the chief of police, where persons to whom privilege of parading on public streets would be accorded was left within uncontrolled official discretion of chief of police and no standard of regulating constitutional provision that no state shall deprive any person of life, liberty, or property without "due process of law" nor deny any person "equal protection of the law." '35 C.S.A. c.163, ~ 10,subd. 7; U.S.c.a. Const. Amend. 14, ~ 1.

See Words and Phrases, Permanent Edition, for all other definitions of "Due Process of Law" and Equal Protection of the Law".

En Banc.

Error to Huerfano County Court; Joseph A. Barron, Judge.

Robert Trujillo, Toney Trujillo and Maurico Romero, plaintiffs in error, to whom we hereinafter refer as defendants, were charged in separate complaints with the violation of ordinance No. 273 of the City of Walsenburg, in that they "did unlawfully use the street of the City of Walsenburg by using said streets for the purpose of parading and organizing a procession without securing a permit from the chief of police of said city as provided by said ordinance." The pertinent language of the ordinance, upon which these charges are based, is as follows: "Section 1. That it shall be unlawful for any person or persons or association to use the streets of the City of Walsenburg, Colorado for any parade, processions or street assemblage without first obtaining a permit from the Chief of Police of the City of Walsenburg so to do."

Defendants, upon trial to the court, were found guilty of violating the ordinance in question and fined, the fines being suspended upon payment of costs, judgment for which was entered against them. Since there was no record of the testimony taken at the trial, counsel for both sides entered into a written stipulation setting forth the facts, which, briefly, are as follows:

Defendants and others, after being refused a permit, paraded and assembled, without a permit, on the sidewalks of Walsenburg February 21, 1940, about sixty persons participating in the procession walking three abreast, and some were carrying signs.

There was no violence and the others dispersed peaceably; defendants admitted on the trial that they had violated the terms of the ordinance, but asserting its unconstitutionality, they offered no testimony; the evidence disclosed that at different times in the past parades and assemblages were held in the City of Walsenburg by other organizations, permits therefor having been issued by the proper authority; that defendants are members of an organization known as the Workers' Alliance.

Defendants contend that the ordinance in question is invalid, in that it violates the following provisions of section 1 of the Fourteenth Amendment to the Constitution of the United States, which provides that: "No State shall make or enforce any law which shall abridge the privileges or immunities of citizens of the United States; nor shall any State deprive any person of life, liberty, or property, without due process of law; nor deny to any person within its jurisdiction the equal protection of the laws." The specific point of unconstitutionality asserted is that the ordinance is void on its face because under its provisions the chief of police of the city may arbitrarily grant or refuse a permit for any parade, procession or street assemblage. No standards of official action are set up in the ordinance under which the designated official, without discrimination, may grant permits. His authority to grant permits—which is not expressly conferred by the ordinance—depends primarily upon his personal opinion or desire, uncircumscribed by any legislative standard of control.

[1] The power of municipalities, under our state law, to regulate the use of public streets is conceded. '35 C.S.A., chapter 163, section 10, subparagraph 7. "The privilege of a citizen of the United States to use the streets *** may be regulated in the interest of all; it is not absolute, but relative, and must be exercised in subordination to the general comfort and convenience, and in consonance with peace and good order; but it must not, in the guise of regulation, be abridged or denied." Hague, Mayor, v. Committee for Industrial Organization, 307 U.S. 496, 516, 59 S.C.Ct. 954, 964, 83 L. Ed. 1423.

[2,3] An excellent statement of the power of a municipality to impose regulations in the use of public streets if found in the recent case of Cox v. New Hampshire, 312 U.S. 569, 61 S.Ct. 762, 765,85 L.Ed. 1049, 133 A.L.R. 1396, in which the following appears: "The authority of a municipality to impose regulations in order to assure the safety and convenience of the people in the use of public highways has never been regarded as inconsistent with civil liberties but rather as one of the means of safeguarding the good order upon which they ultimately depend. The control of travel on the streets of cities is the most familiar illustration of this recognition of social need. Where a

relation is designed to promote the public convenience in the interest of all, it cannot be disregarded by the attempted exercise of some civil right which in other circumstances would be entitled to protection. One would not be justified in ignoring the familiar red traffic light because he thought it his religious duty to disobey the municipal command or sought by that means to direct public attention to an announcement of his opinions. As regulation of the use of the streets for parades and processions is a traditional exercise of control by local government, the question in a particular case is whether that control is exerted so as not to deny or unwarrantedly abridge the right of assembly and the opportunities for the communication of thought and the discussion of public questions immemorially associated with resort to public places. Lovell v. Griffin, 303 U.S. 444, 451, 58 S. Ct. 666, 668, 82 L.Ed. 949 [953]; Hague v. Committee for industrial Organization, 307 U.S. 496, 515, 516, 59 S. Ct. 954, 963, 964, 83 L.Ed, 1423 [1436, 1437]; Schneider v. State of New Jersey [Town of Irvington], 308 U.S. 147, 160, 60 S.Ct. 146, 150, 84 L. Ed, 155 [164]; Cantwell v. Connecticut, 310 U.S. 296, 306, 307, 60 S.Ct. 900, 904, 84 L Ed. 1213 [1219, 1220], 128 A.L.R. 1352."

[4] Our concern here is the validity or non-validity of an ordinance which leaves to the uncontrolled official discretion of the chief of police if a municipal corporation to say who shall, and who shall not, be accorded the privilege of parading on its public streets. No standard of regulation is even remotely suggested. Moreover, under the ordinance as drawn, the chief of police may for any reason, which he may entertain arbitrarily, deny this privilege to any group. This is authorization of the exercise of arbitrary power by a government agency, which violates the Fourteenth Amendment. People v. Harris, 104 Colo. 386, 394, 91 P.2d 989, 122 A.L.R. 1034. Such an ordinance is unreasonable and void on its face. City of Chicago v. Trotter, 136 1430, 26 N.E. 359. See, also, Anderson v. City of Wellington, 40 Kan. 173, 19 P. 719, 2 L.R.A. 110, 10 Am.St. Rep.175; State ex rel. v. Dering, 84 Wis. 585, 54 N.W. 1104, 19 L.R.A. 858,36 Am. St. Rep. 948; Anderson, v. Tedford, 80 Fla. 376, 85 So. 673, 10 A.L.R. 1481; State v. Coleman, 96 Conn. 190, 113 A. 385, 387; 43 C.J., p. 419, ~549; 44 C.J., p. 1036, ~3885. In

the case of Hague, Mayor, v. Committee for Industrial Organization, supra, the Supreme Court of the United States had before it the question of whether an ordinance authorizing the director of public safety of a city to refuse to issue a permit for the use of the public streets, "for the purpose of preventing riots, disturbances or disorderly assemblage," was unconstitutional on its face and therefore void. Mr. Justice Roberts, in an opinion which he delivered in the case, stated his views in the following language (pages 515, 516 of 307 U.S., page 946 of 59 S.Ct, 83 L.Ed. 1423):

"Wherever the title of streets and parks may rest, they have immemorially been held in trust for the use of the public and, time out of mind, have been used for purposes of assembly, communicating thoughts between citizens, and discussing public questions. Such use of the streets and public places has, from ancient times, been a part of the privileges, immunities, rights, and liberties of citizens. The privilege of a citizen of the United States to use the streets and parks for communication of views on national questions may be regulated in the interest of all; it is not absolute, but relative, and must be exercised in subordination to the general comfort and convenience, and in consonance with peace and good order; but it must not, in the guise of regulation, be abridged or denied.

"We think the court below was right in holding the ordinance quoted in Note 1 void upon its face. It does not make comfort or convenience in the use of streets or parks the standard of official action. It enables the Director of Safety to refuse a permit on his mere opinion that such refusal will prevent 'riots, disturbances or disorderly assemblage.'

It can thus, as the record discloses, be made the instrument of arbitrary suppression of free expression of views on national affairs for the prohibition of all speaking will undoubtedly 'prevent' such eventualities. But uncontrolled official suppression of the privilege cannot be made a substitute for the duty to maintain order in connection with the exercise of the right."

The court held the ordinance involved to be unconstitutional and void, notwithstanding the previous action of the Supreme Court of the state of New Jersey in Thomas v. Casey,

121 N.J.L. 185, 1 A.2d 866, in which it held the same ordinance to be valid, stating in its opinion that the issuance of the permit rested in the sound discretion of the director of safety, a municipal officer.

In the instant case the uncontrolled official suppression of the privilege of using the public streets in a lawful manner clearly is apparent from the face of the ordinance before us, and we therefore hold it null and void.

Nothing we have here said is to be construed as holding that a municipality may not properly regulate the use of its streets within constitutional limitations. Such was the holding in the Cox v. New Hampshire case. There the construction placed upon the statutory regulation under consideration, as stated by the New Hampshire court. State v. Cox, 91 N.11. 137, 16 A.2d 508, and quoted by the United States Court, was that, "The defendants *** had a right, under the act, to a license to march when, where and as they did, if after a required investigation it was found that the convenience of the public in the use of the streets would not thereby be unduly disturbed, upon such conditions or changes in time, place and manner as would avoid disturbance." The ordinance before us does not permit of such a construction. Moreover, we here are not concerned with state statutes or municipal ordinances which, under the police power, expressly declare unlawful the use of streets under certain circumstances, without violating our traditional civil liberties. Liberty does not extend to actions, all or a part of which consist of processions on public streets by unauthorized military or semimilitary units, whose conduct is evidence of a clear and present danger to the existence of our democratic institutions, or the purpose of which is to subvert the constitutionally established procedures for the succession of power within the state.

The judgment is reversed and the case remanded with directions to dismiss the complaints.

FRANCIS E. BOUCK, C., J., not participating.

The following are clips of each one of the Denver 14:

It describes the background of each of the demonstrators, together with a sentence or so from each as to his or her motivation for participating in the sit-in.

JAMES DI BERARDINIS, 27…social worker…bom Downington, Pa…. Graduate of St. Joseph's College, Philadelphia, 1964…served in Peace Corps in Santiago, Chile 1964-1966…spent two years as trainer of VISTA volunteers for Westinghouse Learning Corp…. working with Council of the Drums in Denver. "My purpose for entering the Senate Chamber was to express my dissatisfaction with the injustices inflicted by our American system of government and to call fellow citizens to the cause of justice for all men."

JUDY FEZLER, 21…student…from Brainerd, Minn…. Transferred from University of Minnesota to University of Colorado—Denver Center with major in sociology…has worked with American Indian programs and with Awareness Now Program for the disadvantaged…active in working for farm labor legislation in Colorado. "I took part in the Senate sit-in because of my interest in helping people who are forced to live under subhuman conditions. In Colorado I found that after all other methods had been tried and didn't work, the only peaceful means to continue was in the action we took."

FATHER CRAIG HART, 30…assistant pastor, Annunciation Parish, Denver…born Salida, Colo….Graduate of Colorado College, Colorado Springs…Graduate of Saint Thomas Seminary, Denver…teaches religion at St. Joseph High School, Denver, Colorado. "I did this particular 'thing' because of the disastrous silence of too many people who ought to be saying and doing something for the future of people."

MRS. PORTIA HITCHENS, 44… director, ClearingHouse for Concerned Citizens…stockbroker's wife…bom Saint Clair Shores, Mich…. Educated in Detroit schools and by her father who had three doctorates but didn't believe in college. Interior Decorator…has been on boards of Channel 6, Urban Coalition, League of Women Voters, and The Denver Art Museum. "I felt that the proper legislative procedures had been rendered ineffective by the fact the legislators had not been representing their constituents."

MISS SHEILA IVERS, 24...parish worker at Annunciation Parish, Denver...from Salt Lake City...Educated Marillac College, Normandy, Mo., and University of Utah...surgical nurse... former nun, Daughters of the Cross, Sheveport, La.... helped start well-baby clinic for the poor in Salt Lake City... has taught religion at Cathedral High School. "I feel that the legislature has been much more violent in killing 22 bills which could have alleviated many of the problems arising today through social apathy, prejudice and misunderstanding, and perpetrated attitudes that are to me totally unchristian."

JAMES GARCIA 32...civil rights specialist, formerly with Colorado Civil Rights Commission...native Denverite...Graduate of University of Colorado in political science...has been director, Jobs For Progress...past coordinator, New Hispano Movement...candidate for mayor of Denver, 1967...currently with Consultants in Human Resources, Inc. "I was damn sick and tired of marching and picketing and felt that only a dramatic demonstration such as the action taken by the 'Denver 14' would provide the necessary stimulus to motivate other middleclass people into taking similar type action.

FATHER LAWRENCE MARTIN JENCO, 34...assistant pastor, Assumption Parish, Welby, Colo...born Joliet, 111...studied philosophy in Riverside, Calif Studied theology in Rome, Italy...postgraduate work at Catholic University, Washington, D.C....taught in minor seminary in Elgin, taught high school religion at Mt. Carmel, Denver....plans to form communication center with fellow priests in the Order of Servants of Mary on the West Coast. "I became involved because people today are apathetic and indifferent to the many social ills that plague our state. You don't need a political theory to follow—just open up your eyes and see the problems. Many of our people feel that Christian teaching has nothing to do with social issues. Somehow the Gospel has been white-washed."

WILLIAM M. MILLER, 23, Student, "presently celebrating life in the Spirit"...former student at St. Thomas College and Seminary, Denver...served in U.S. Marine Corps for three years. "My motivation? According to many wise holy men we must respond to human suffering, feed the poor and follow that positive law and commandment of love. I, feel I was responding to the Spirit."

RAMON NAVARRO, 32...consultant, Center for urban Affairs, CU...Student at CU Denver Center...born Sweetwater, Tex....dropped out of school after 7th grade...later earned high school diploma...several years at optical trade in Denver... case worker, counselor, trainer with Job Opportunity Center, Denver. "You get awfully frustrated after all those months and years of trying to get people to do the right thing."

MISS JUNE REEVES, 23...1969 Graduate of Loretto Heights College, degree in behavioral sciences...staff member of Turnstile, center for runaway youth...was student coordinator of social action in college...served with Action Toward Suburban Involvement and Vision program in Littleton last summer. "I hoped there were still people around who could read that 14 people were willing to be arrested following a non-violent action to prove a point and that would start them thinking."

LENO ROMERO, 25...technician at Honeywell Corp...Student at Metro State College...born Platteville, Colo...Graduate of West High School, Denver. "My basic motivation was just one thing: I knew that people needed help and I wanted to give it where it would have some impact."

SISTER PATRICIA SEAL, 22...staff member at Auraria Community Center, Denver...A Sister of Loretto...native of Denver... Graduate of Machebeuf High School, Denver... graduate of Loretto Heights College, 1969. "I was discouraged with asking the legislature to listen. We've tried every other means and finally felt we had to do this."

ROBERT TRUJILLO, 65...retired cement contractor...born Chama, Colo...coal miner in Walsenburg in '20s... WPA in '30s...farm laborer for a dollar a day in '40s...joined Communist Party in '30s, still active. "I believe that my action in the Colorado Senate on May 7 only expressed my deep concern for all the people and hoping that the people in general will speak out against injustices committed by our present way of running things."

THE REV. AUSTIN "MACK' WARNER, 49...former director, Ministry of Urban Concern, Colorado Council of Churches... born Fort Gibson, Miss...high school education, Abilene, Tex...Texas Christian University, B.A. 1947...Brite Divinity School, B.D. 1950...Union Theological Seminary S.T.M. 1961... artillery officer World War II 1942-1945...minister in Dallas 1950-1951... missionary in Japan 1951–1956...administrator in New York City Protestant Council for 10 years. "We did what we did to lift up before the state legislature and the people that almost every bill that would help to alleviate some of the poverty and injustice was killed in committee." (Alexander Rev., "Why 14 Seized The Colorado Senate In May," *The Denver Post*, 12 July 1969.)

POEMS FROM MY STORY

Me
I have to talk to someone so bad,
I have to tell what makes me sad,
I have to get things off my chest,
So that my heavy heart can rest.

I just found out who I can tell and
Sometimes, it is hell!
Peace of mind seems hard to find,
Yet it is there every-time.
For only I can understand, for only
I know who I am.   *Mary Lou Salazar*

Walk
Walk a mile in my shoes.
Take a trip through my mind.
View the world with my perception—
Take the time.

Walk a mile in my shoes.
Spend a day, spend more time.
Judge me because I am afraid, because I
do not trust easily.

Walk a mile in my shoes; spend the night with my thoughts—
Listens closely hear me cry—feel the hope inside me die.

Walk a mile in my shoes.
Feel the love that's deep inside.
Feel me come alive as,
I touch humanity.

Walk a mile in my shoes.
Feel the love that's been suppressed.
Feel the love that society's forced
me to regress to childhood alienation.

Feel the anger move within because
my love has a right to be.
Feel the under current that's deep within.
Walk a mile in my shoes
Feel the love that's stirs within.

Feel the joy I feel because your
by my side.

Walk a mile in my shoes.   *Mary Lou Salazar*

My Culture
My culture, my life,
The essence of me,

the roots so deep inside of me.
The values I keep,
from memories I weep.

The need for freedom,
the need for love,
the heart that leads me
back to my blood.

The quest for identity,
the search for the truth,
all brings me home,
to my roots.   Mary Lou Salazar

The Rebel
They call me a rebel!
I rebel against evil,
against lies, against hate,
against feeble minded elites.
I rebel against hate crimes, against
fools, against games, against pain.

I rebel against injustice,
against wars that are filled with deceit, with
profit motives,
that kills humanity.

I rebel with those who dare not to sleep, who
dare to hope,
and revolt for love.

I rebel against you, because you don't give a damn
that humanity dies
right before your eyes and
because it's not you or those close to you—
you ignore the truth and go on.

I read the truth looking deep in your eyes.
I rebel against people, who are afraid to live,

because they're afraid to die and
afraid to die, because they're afraid to live.

Do you enjoy when it turns inside?
When the lies are within you and
you can't even move? And you die while your
body appears to be alive.

I rebel in the name of justice,
of truth, of love.
I rebel in the name of hope
that I move you to care—
And give hope to the children everywhere!   Mary Lou Salazar

Determination
Over a mountain, across the sea, I'm seeing the sun,
then a huge mountain before me.
I have to climb once again.
I'll do it alone, because I've done it
before and I'll do it again.

There's not much sun at the foot of the hill, but I'll see it soon
by fighting with my strong will.

Determination is the key,
persistence and patience
are a part of me.

Love is my reason for living.
Faith in mankind gives me strength.
Laughter and joy help me move.
Courage and the desire to change make me free.
Revolution (change) is my life, join me.   Mary Lou Salazar

Time and Space
Time and space
I ran the race.
I've paid my dues.

I walked miles
in your shoes.

Time and space
I won one race.
I made the top,
A Ph.D.
But no job to
go with me.
Time and space
I ran the race.
Oh what the hell!
I did it well.

I married the love of my life.
I raised three beautiful children.
Who all ran their race
in their own time and space.
I am blessed with six beautiful
grandchildren, eight great grandchildren who I hope
to reach.

I still teach!

I teach not the traditional way
I teach and reach you
In your time and space.   Mary Lou Salazar

Tomorrow
Tomorrow is unknown to me.
Who I am now is not who I'll be.
I'm waiting, I'm moving towards
the sea.

I'm creative, destructive, emotional, and intellectual
I'm hard to beat down.

I'll still be around while the weaker ones cry
I'll still be here after others die.

Can't spend a lifetime on being meek!
Can't spend a moment on being weak!

I don't want to be aggressive and make others feel small.
I want to be loving and sensitive and make others feel tall.
                                    Mary Lou Salazar

Articles, Letters and Excerpts

Many of my father, Robert Trujillo's, predictions still fit the conditions in the United States today, such as the danger of police brutality. The March 6, 2000, edition of *TIME* magazine cover stories are "COPS BRUTALITY & RACE- "The Diallo Verdict" and "The LAPD Scandal." Both illustrate the fact that racism and police brutality and corruption are very much alive in the new millennium. Chua-Eoan, Howard, writes an article in *Time* magazine "BLACK & BLUE" -The four cops who killed Amadoou Diallo are acquitted, but the case will go on raising questions about race and crime fighting, sending tremors right through the November elections. THE FOUR-WHITE POLICEMAN HAD FIRED 41 bullets at the young African immigrant; 19 hit their mark." Chua-Eoan, Howard. "Black and Blue." *Time* magazine March 6, 2000.

Adam Cohen writes in *Time* magazine, "Gangsta COPS" As the >P>D> scandal keeps growing, a city asks itself, "How could the police have gone so bad?" So what have you got for us? It's the question D.S.'s always throw back at criminals looking to save their own hides. O.K., then what bigger fish are you going to help us fry?

In this case the prep cop, Rafael Perez, was a Los Angeles cop accused of stealing 6 lbs. of cocaine from downtown headquarters to sell on the street. If Perez wanted to plea- bargain that, he'd better offer something pretty good.

He did. Perez admitted that he and his partner had shot an unarmed, handcuffed 19-year- old and planted a rifle on him to cover it up. And then, in 2,000 pages of riveting testimony, Perez yanked back on a dark, dime-store-novel world in which cops routinely frame the innocent by planting ("throwing down") drugs and guns, smack around)"thump") citizens on the street for kicks and perjure themselves ("join the liar's club") to get convictions. Cohen, Adam "GANGSTA COPS." *Time* magazine. 6 March 2000.

The Denver 14 Defense Committee' released the following statement:

The Denver 14 Defense Committee

We support and defend the demonstration of the Denver 14 in the Colorado State Legislature for these reasons:

An action of this sort was vitally necessary to bring before the state legislature an urgent appeal to halt its rush for adjournment and reconsider favorably the numerous bills it had killed affecting farm labor, consumer protection, housing, police and justice, education and welfare.

Every available means of expressing the imperative needs for corrective legislation on behalf of the disadvantaged were used to the maximum throughout the entire session, but to no avail. The legislators had been made aware of the urgent necessity for the passage of these bills by combined attempts at labor negotiation, boycotts, numerous petitions, peaceful picketing of the legislature, lobbying, subcommittee testimony, and direct appeals to the legislature.

Through this dramatic use of "body rhetoric" to express the people's voice where it had gone consistently unheeded throughout the entire 47th General Assembly, thousands of citizens of Colorado have also been made acutely aware—many for the first time—that over 20 bills to meet human needs were killed. This fact is now better understood, and many people of good will, who simply did not know how callously the legislature treated the poor, will now be better informed and more eager to work for the needed changes in social legislation.

This was an entirely non-violent action by the Denver 14. It was directed toward better conditions for ALL Colorado citizens. These fouorteen people deserve your support.

Why 14 Seized the Colorado Senate in May

In 1969 Alexander Rev. Paul S. writes, "Why 14 Seized the Colorado Senate in May." *The Denver Post* "(Mr. Alexander is minister of the United Church of the Applewoods, Golden.) On Wednesday, May 7, an unprecedented event took place in the chambers of the Colorado State. A group of 14 demonstrators barged their way into the chambers—they had not realized in advance the Senate was in closed session—and took over the presiding officer's platform. There they made a number of speeches protesting the lack of social legislation passed in the 47th General Assembly.

This event was variously reported in the press. My own interest in the event developed initially out of the fact that I knew some of the 14 on a personal basis.

As I learned more about this group two factors impressed me: 1: Their diversity of background, talents and motivation: 2. The amount of time and effort they had spent as individuals working through "the proper channels" to gain social legislation.

Who Broke the Law

This letter, Who Broke the Law? came out in *The Denver Catholic Register,* 1970. "Catholics for a Better Society, at a meeting last week, issued a statement denouncing the corrupt influences at work in the state legislature, and the complete failure on the part of the legislature to understand or to listen to the strident voices of the poor and of the middle class who are without powerful [lobbies] to aid them. The focal point of criticism was the legislature's callous consignment of farm workers to second class citizenship. The assembly refused to extend to these workers coverage under the Colorado Labor Peace Act and imposed restrictive qualification requirements for their coverage under Workman's Compensation and Unemployment Insurance. Members agreed that this rejection of modest and reasonable legislation designed to help the poor help themselves provoked the sit-in, which occurred in the Senate Chamber.

There are those who reproach the 14 dedicated people who violated, in a peaceful manner, the rules of the Senate. Whether their methods are acceptable is a matter for private judgment.

It is the worst sort of hypocrisy for those who speak piously of law and order to stand by and watch a lawmaking body violate the rules of human decency, perpetrating injustice and wholly ignoring the needs of its people. We therefore support fully the purpose of the protest and will aid the group in every way possible on the charges they face."

Don Burton, Chairman
Catholics for a Better Society
Denver

In 1980 Dad writes this letter to Editorial writer, Fred Brown.

Point of View Original Copy

Robert Trujillo, Chairman
Colorado Communist Party
March 27, 1980

Historic March 6, 1930
Fifty years ago, on March 6, 1930, to be exact, United States workers changed history. They took another giant step which, in historic importance, ranks with the Haymarket demonstration for the eight-hour day and the CIO. Drive to organize the basic, mass production industries.

On March 6, 1930, at least 1,250,000 workers rallied, despite arrests and bloody police attacks, in the streets of cities and industrial centers, including Denver, demanding "work or wages," jobs or relief. Initiated by the Communist Party, Unemployed Councils and the Trade Union Unity League, the demonstrations opened a new stage of workers' struggles in which workers demanded recognition of their rights by the ruling class and the government.

Out of this there developed a new relationship and also the fights for implementation of the rights of workers to unemployment compensation, Social Security Pensions, and legal rights of trade unions.

Big business and government did not give anything without resisting. All of labor's rights and gains had to be fought for.

And the workers of the 1930s fought courageously, militantly in such an organized and class-conscious way that workers today, and the nation as well, benefit.

In calling for the March 6th demonstration, the Communist Party distributed one million leaflets in New York City alone. It had already helped to organize the Unemployed Councils, which later organized two National Hunger Marches on Washington.

The powerful impact of the March 6th demonstration was amplified by the fact that they were part of an international working class "Don't Starve: Fight:" answer to the gigantic capitalist world crisis. Communist Parties in many countries simultaneously led great mass demonstrations on March 6th.

March 6th will one day be named a working class holiday. In the mean time, the gains from the movement it sparked still benefit all workers, all retired people and those at the very bottom of the economic ladder, and it stands as an outstanding example of how workers' and all common peoples struggles can change history.

The March 6 demonstrations hold a major lesson for today. Labor can fight and win on basic issues, even during hard times.

In 1930, 25 percent of the workers were jobless and Franklin Delano Roosevelt said he was saving capitalism from collapse. Workers did not beg, they demanded. They did not let themselves be intimidated by police violence or big business pressure, or be divided by red baiting. The workers fought and won.

Today with inflation and unemployment mounting, plants closing, and Washington putting the screws on the people; congress proposing for the elimination of annual cost of living adjustments, for reduction of federal funds for the poor while at the same time increasing the military budget to $156 billion under the trumped-up excuse of the Soviet Union's so-called "invasion" of Afghanistan and the Iranian crisis. There is only one solution and one answer: ORGANIZE AND FIGHT AGAINST THE MADNESS AND INSANE GREED OF THE BIG CORPORATIONS IN THIS NATION!

If President Jimmy Carter and Congress are really sincere about Human Rights in other parts of the world, how come they keep silent about the violent actions, the racist preaching of groups such as the Klu Klux Klan? How come not a single Presidential Candidate of the two major parties addresses the real issues facing our nation?

The Communist Party USA has Gus Hall running for President and Angela Davis running for Vice-President this year. They speak out for-full employment, no cuts on funding for the social needs of the people, stopping the drive toward a third world war, reducing the excessive and outrageous profits of Big Business, by stopping and reducing the inflationary prices that go up and up every day! By putting a stop on the drug traffic that destroys the minds of our young every day.

These are the things that our government needs to do in our country. Not trying to police the world for the benefit of those infested with greed.

Even our own little Governor Dick Lamm should quit thinking of taking over little Socialist Cuba. Let us unite and solve the problems in these beloved United States of America.

Sincerely,

Robert Trujillo
C/O Mr. Fred Brown
Editorial Writer
The Denver, Post

Negative Press
Responding to Robert Trujillo's letter "Point of View" *The Denver Post* **12 March 1980.**

Target of the communist' big lie: gullible target groups

"I must grant the communists one thing: They are absolutely unsurpassed when it comes to colossal, raw, unmitigated gall. Robert Trujillo's letter (Point of View March 27) is a case in point. Trujillo, the chairman of the Colorado Communist Party, would like you to believe his party is a friend of the workers. He rants about "police violence," big business pressure," increasing the military budget," "insane greed of big corporations" and the trumped-up excuse of the Soviet Union's so-called invasion of Afghanistan.

On the other hand, he applauds the "right of workers to unemployment compensation, Social Security pensions, and legal rights' of trade unions."

Yet:

Over the last 20 years or so, U.S. courts have steadily tightened the rules guaranteeing the rights of the accused. Any policeman found guilty of a transgression against the law is subject to reprimand by his superiors and to criminal and civil penalties.

In Trujillo's beloved Soviet Union and its colonies, beatings by government thugs, long-term detention without trial, denial of needed medical care and occasional sudden disappearance of the critics of the regime are quite common. (In Czechoslovakia, several people were recently sentenced to prison for pointing out publicly that in certain cases, people had unjustly persecuted in violation of Czechoslovak laws.)

COMRADE TRUJILLO objects to the increase in the U.S. military budget. We have been slashing ours to the bone for years while the Soviets tripled theirs.

We have some 19 divisions in the entire U.S. Army and the Marines; the Soviets have added about 25 over the last few years and now have 177 divisions.

Trujillo talks of peace, yet virtually every war since the '40s was started or incited by the communists.

People like Trujillo, Jane Fonda and Angela Davis told us that peace would return to Southeast Asia as soon as the bad Americans were kicked out by the good communists. We abandoned our allies there to the Reds, but peace did not return.

I KNOW one can't convince a 72-year-old communist.

There is one virtually unfailing cure for them, namely, have them live under the system for a year or two as an ordinary citizen, not as a visiting red dignitary from the West.

There are fewer dedicated communists in Prague today than in Denver. Communism is like measles: Once you have been through it, you become immune. But Trujillo won't take the cure.

Comrade Trujillo may yet get his wish.

If the U.S. government and some businessmen whose greed is exceeded only by their naivete continue to support the Soviet Union by a steady stream of money, food and technology, and if the U.S. government continues to undercut our friends in the world, the United States will become a "socialist paradise" before very long (unless we get incinerated by a Soviet first strike).

But that would be a tragedy for him. As the economy of the world collapses (there won't be any capitalist United States then to make up for the incompetence of socialism), Trujillo will have to explain to his own children and grandchildren, expendable serfs of the all-powerful state that this was the dream he has been promoting all his life.

I knew quite a few old, idealistic ex-communists in Czechoslovakia whose children asked that question. Some of them hanged themselves.

I do not envy comrade Trujillo." **Letters to the Editor**

In June, 1969 D. L. Herndon HMI, *The Denver Post* writes:

Reply to Trujillo on Senate March

Would you please inform the "self proclaimed" Communist Robert Trujillo that the Colorado Senate and the House of Representatives offers a far more cross section of representation to the citizens of Colorado than his group of so called dissident youths.

Our legislative body was elected by the people. Evidently Trujillo and his group have not got the word yet. His trooping into the Senate with his mob following was cheap, sordid theatrical and certainly failed to impress the group he came to humiliate. He accomplished far more however. That is to outrage our feelings for the interruption of peaceful and free assembly which is something many Americans including myself are here in Vietnam fighting for this very day. We see his type over here every day. Even the local villagers would recognize his line. I hope, God I hope, you, the citizens of Denver, do no fall for it.

Trujillo is the type that exploits the poor and disadvantaged, not helping them. His type feeds on the problems and ills of the unfortunate, not create new life or help for them. He's certainly not constructive. Why? Simple. All he would have had to have done to be heard was to have used the U.S. Mail Service in naming out his complaints.

I say Trujillo's methods and the groups like his that hung around colleges, high schools and neighborhoods protesting and not helping cure the ills are only a phase, a phase that the good honest American citizens will destroy as it has with all the other plagues we have survived.

The community is a strong bond, it and it alone will cure its ills. Cheap and easy methods without law and justice will never answer the ill or create its replacement.

As a serviceman and a citizen of Denver, I say to all of you of my community don't fall short of the greatness you are capable of. Denver, as well as the rest of America, has a great future as long as we recognize the type that would steal our freedom and rights from us. Good luck Denver. When I get out next year, I'm coming home to help you build, as a lot of other Denver guys are going to do also.

D. L. Herndon HMI,
Medical Department Representative of North Vietnam

My additional Story

My oldest daughter said to me once, "Mom, I think you were born with self-confidence." But I think it had to do with me being socialized to value the truth. My father said love and truth were the same. My father always gave me eye contact. He told me I was very smart and strong. He also allowed me to debate with him and I developed a very strong will. I didn't fear him. Some of my older siblings rebelled against his authority in different ways, but I stood up to him and he allowed me to do so. This was the advantage of being the youngest daughter. As one of the younger children, I reaped the benefit of that privilege quite often throughout my life.

For instance, one time when I was very young and we were all sitting around the kitchen table having supper and Dad was sharing with us about how hard the Depression years had been. He said, "We had so many kids and I was always worried about how I was going to feed all of you." I interrupted him and I said, "Daddy, why in the world did you and Mommy keep making love when you already had so many kids and you couldn't even feed the ones you had?" He got kind of shocked and I saw him grin a little and he answered, "Well, we had nothing else we could do." My siblings chuckled.

Cultural Shock

I spoke only Spanish until I started kindergarten but, once I entered the public school, I experienced cultural shock. I was quickly taught to speak only English. I recall really struggling to learn English. I would lay awake at night struggling to learn the words. I would say "witch watch" for wristwatch and I couldn't pronounce soup I would say "toup." I practiced words way into the night. I swore that someday I would speak English so well that even God would listen to me. I kept my primary language, but I spoke it less and less as I was growing up. So, without even knowing how or when I started speaking only English. Furthermore, not only was the language foreign to me, the entire educational system and culture was foreign to me and it placed me at a disadvantage because I had to study twice as hard as my classmates. Yet I received top grades in elementary and middle school.

1947

Then, as if that wasn't hard enough, in some of my classes the belief that communists were evil was taught. It was 1947 and laws were already passed to outlaw the Communist Party and its members. Like my little brother, I knew at a young age that we were very different. I also knew that they were misinformed. In fact, I knew from my experience that they were wrong. My father was very smart. For example, he taught us about discrimination. He said, "Dogs in our country received better treatment then Mexicans, Blacks and other people of color." He told us kids not to worship and salute the flag of the United States because, as he explained, "If there is a God, why would he bless only America? What about the rest of the world?" I remember sitting when we were instructed in school to stand up and salute the flag. My father explained to us the root causes of racism, classism, discrimination, war and injustices that were well rooted into our history and the development of our country. One teacher asked me why I did not salute the flag and I told him why. Others did not ask me. We were not taught to hate the system but we were taught to expose and help change all the injustices.

I was six years old and we had a friend, who was white, Mr. Berman who always came to visit us and he brought us kids a lot of candy. We just loved him for it. One time a young Mexican named Ruben Valdez was found hanged in the Buena Vista Reformatory and Mr. Berman joined us in a mass protest march. We were marching against the penal institution that the Communist Party claimed was responsible for his death. I mention Mr. Berman because white people were very much a part of our lives. Progressive thinkers were not just minorities. In fact many times we had more white people in the Communist Party than Mexicans and Blacks.

Dad related the Valdez incident to a friend: "Because of the murder of Ruben Valdez, a fifteen-year-old Chicano, we organized a demonstration at the governor's office in downtown Denver, Colorado. He refused to meet with us and we found out that he went out another exist of his office to avoid us. So we organized a demonstration at his private home. That night as we were demonstrating in front of the governor's home, nineteen of us were arrested and we went to jail. The people who supported us were having a hard time getting people to put up bond for us. Then one friend put up bond for me and got me out. And then they got me to put up my property as bonds for the remaining eighteen people. We had a trial and they charged us with unlawful assemblage. We were found guilty. I don't remember how many penalties they gave us. We appealed our case and we went back to court again. Judge Flannagan, a Black judge, presided at the trial and we were acquitted."

My father was always at meetings, organizing, lecturing, speaking out, trying to effect change. At times I went with him. We were buddies. He knew that I knew what he was doing was absolutely necessary. He was my big powerful Daddy who laid down the foundation for others to follow. On the nights that he was gone, my mother and I laid in bed together and we prayed. She asked God to take care of him, to protect all of her children and to bring home safe my oldest brother, Frank, who was a sailor in the United States Navy and was stationed overseas.

When Frank came home from Guam he was walking me to school on a cold snowy day and he said, "Hija, (honey) don't you have any mittens?" I said "No." There was a five and ten cent store on the block where we lived. He went inside the store and bought me soft pink mittens. I was so excited because I had never had a pair of mittens before. God I loved Frank for doing that for me. I felt really special.

Once while in high school I received an F in a class called American Problems because I constantly spoke out against all the lies the teachers fed us. For example, I asked the teacher why we (the Mexicans) are discriminated against here in the United States, but when our young minorities go to war they are not discriminated against. In fact they are on the front line of the battlefield. Then they give their families medals of honor and call them heroes after they are dead. And if they return home alive they can't even get a decent job. But the propaganda works well because our young men keep joining up to go to the service.

My mother's brother died in the San Luis Valley and, at the rosary, the priest along with the people prayed the Holy Mary. "Holy Mary, Mother of God, pray for us sinners now and at the hour of our death." In the Catholic Religion they repeat this prayer over and over. My father whispered to me, "Listen to the psychology behind the words. Pray for us sinners now and at the hour of our death. See, they teach people that we are sinners, that we are bad, not ok, that we have no power, that we must submit and be passive because we need to be saved. Rather than to teach people that God helps those who help themselves and to stand up for our rights and demand justice, the church teaches them to only pray and things will change."

According to Alan Katz, staff writer for *Denver Magazine*, "Oddly, Trujillo admits that he'd be less partisan if he lived in the Soviet Union. He seems to enjoy the antagonistic relationship he has with society, saying 'If I lived in a socialist country,' said Trujillo, 'I would be willing to criticize whatever weaknesses I could detect.' Katz, "True Believer," *Denver Magazine*, January, 1982.

My Story

There were so many of us kids at home and we were poor so Mom always made our dresses. She made them out of flour sacks that my father bought. One time she had some brand new white towels and she made me a beautiful soft white coat with silk lining. I remember feeling so special. I felt like the prettiest girl in school. My mom always told me not to show off even if she told me I looked pretty.

I never got any money to pay for the milk and gram crackers that the teacher passed out everyday for the morning break. But when some kid paid the day before and was absent one of us kids who couldn't pay were asked if we wanted the milk and gram crackers. I would raise my hand for the free treat. I recall the taste of that milk. It was delicious! I would drink it real slow so the taste would stay with me.

It wasn't too often that we got a new pair of shoes. My father always took us to the Good Will, a second hand store, to get our shoes because they only cost 25 cents. But one time, when I did get a brand new pair of shoes, even though Mom told me not to look at my shoes all day, I couldn't help myself. Every chance I got I looked at my new pair of oxford shoes.

One winter when I was eleven I got my first new coat. It was blue and really big on me. My father explained that, even though I was small, he had to buy it two sizes bigger than my size. That way, he said, he would not have to buy me a coat for a couple of years. If that were today, I would be picked up as a suspected gang member because it was so big on me. But I didn't care. It sure kept me warm and I loved it even when the other children looked at me strangely.

I did receive two very special gifts when I was a child. I was four years old and my brother, Pete, was twelve and he worked every morning delivering the Rocky Mountain News. He bought me an old doll from the second hand store. It was made of wood. He washed the doll's cloths and he painted her pink. I wondered why he painted it pink when I was brown? (He probably found some old paint in the barn out back). I was thrilled to death and I loved that doll and I loved Pete for giving her to me. It was my baby. Then another time when I was five, my sister, Ruth, was working and she bought the three of us girls' brand new dolls. Mine was a fat baby doll with dark pink rubber pants. I was never so happy in my life. I carried that doll everywhere I went.

When I was in middle school my sister, Orlanda, made me very happy. I was running for president of the 7th grade and she made me a beautiful red cotton skirt and blouse in her sewing class. I had to go on stage before the student body to give my speech. I'm sure she received an A for her grade in sewing, because I think the outfit won me the votes! I was the president of the 7th grade for that year.

As much love as we shared in our family, we were not without problems. My two older brothers Fred, and Gil, left home when they were in their teens. They had a conflict with my father over something that happened at Lakeside Amusement Park where they were working. Anyway, I remember the police coming to our home and my father got real angry with my brothers. Then they moved out on their own. I missed them, but eventually they made up with my dad.

A few years later my sister, Orlanda, ran away and I saw my father crying for the first time. He laid his head on the kitchen table and cried. I was so upset. But she returned in a few days. Some time after that incident she came back home and she went to stay with my brother, Fred and his wife, Julie. Dad learned my brother, Fred had signed for her to be married. She got married when she was fifteen years old against my father's wishes. That created another conflict between my brother, Fred and my father.

My Mother

My mother was an orphan and I'm grateful for her upbringing. She gave me freedom of thought. I believe that, because of her childhood alone with little guidance and socialization, she was able to experience curiosity and self thought. She transferred to me an open beauty of life, sex, wonder, a simple knowledge of and appreciation for life and deep faith, which to me is pure wisdom.

My Father

My father, on the other hand, affected me to cultivate my intellect and to feel responsible for my family and humanity. When I graduated with my BA he gave me a card in which he wrote: "Your mother and I are very proud of you. Now you can help save the world." I thought to myself, "That's going to be a pretty big job!"

My Culture

My culture was the culture of poverty, of being a Mexican, of struggle, of Jesus and Marxism all combined. And somewhere in there I was an American.

The values that I received were: that life has tremendous value; that love is why we are born and why we live. I was taught to value peace and justice. Education is a top priority for me. It was instilled in me that I must get an education, but that I must help people rise from their oppression. Faith is something I have always had. I believe that life has a higher purpose, and that there is much more to life than what the eye can see. I value scientific investigation and research, but I also value the spiritual realm. I was taught and I believe that we must give to life in order to make the world better.

My Mexican Culture

As for being exposed to the arts and the beauty of my Mexican Culture, I feel cheated. I listened to Mexican music a lot but, other than that, I never was exposed too much about my culture. I'm sure it was because we didn't have money to attend cultural events like plays or musicals, but again it didn't seem like there were many cultural events around like there are today. The first time I experienced a play about my people was when I was an adult and I saw a play in a teatro (on stage) educating the audience about the plight of the farm workers.

I didn't attend church except for a funeral or a wedding and, I suppose, that is where in many ways the Mexican Culture is taught. Other than being fluent in Spanish, I really did not have much positive exposure to my Mexican Culture. In fact, I have learned and enjoy more as an adult and I am grateful I kept my native language. Like my brother Frank, I did not teach our children to speak Spanish and I sincerely regret that.

The role models I was exposed to of my people were: Mexicans working as housekeepers, dishwashers, custodians, cooks, garbage collectors, in fact all of the laborers. As a child I never saw a Mexican doctor. I had one teacher who was Mexican in junior high school and he affected me to feel very intelligent. Yet the earlier things I saw around me affected me so much that I allowed a counselor at North High School to convince me that I should go into Home Economics for my major. And that's what I graduated from high school with, a Home Economics major. Nothing is ever wasted: I'm a good cook!

I also experienced discrimination in other subtle and not so subtle ways. When I was about to graduate from high school we had a class called homeroom. We had the same teacher and the same students for the four years we were in high school. Anyway, each of us was asked to stand up and tell the class what our future plans were. When I stood up, I said very proudly that I was getting married two days after graduation. And the teacher said, "Mary Lou always had a lot of potential, but she never used it." I felt terrible!

Years later, when I graduated from college with honors, I received a phone call. The person from the university asked me how and why I received poor grades my senior year in high school and was graduating with honors from the University of Colorado? I told her that during my senior year I was very sick and missed a few weeks of school. And then I mentioned the two incidents: I told her that, actually, my teacher at North High School's, comments in fact affected me to pursue my degree. I thought about her a lot and I said to myself, "I'll show you!" The sad part is I was the only Mexican in the class and I regret that I did not talk back to her.

In graduate school a professor tried to insult me by giving me no grade on my paper. Believe me, I gave her a piece of my mind. She got real nervous when I asserted to her and she said for me not to be so upset: that she would show me how to "jump through the hoops". I replied, "I'm not a monkey and I don't need your charity, and it's too bad that students can't give professors grades because I'd give you an F." I dropped her class after my advisor said I could. She often made sarcastic remarks to me and I got fed up. Again, I was the only Mexican in the class. But this time I have no regrets because I did talk back to her. Even taking the risk that she might try to fail me. It was real satisfying.

My American Culture

As a child the American Culture to me meant materialism, a good education to get ahead, and power to control others. This was not to imply the American Culture had nothing positive to offer, but this was my earliest recollection of it.

My brother, Gil, use to sing like Frank Sinatra. He always sang to us kids and played the harmonica. There were drapes hanging from his bedroom and us kids would sit on the floor and he would pull open the drapes and entertain us. He valued

America and made me proud to be an American. He would sing to us, "The house I live in, the people that I meet, all races, all religions that's American to me."

My brother, Fred, said, "Whenever I travel or see other poor countries, I'm sure happy we were born in American, even though we have many problems to contend with."

When I was a teenager my brother, Fred, would sing to me and play the guitar and have me follow along with him singing in Spanish. It was so much fun babysitting for his children and then I got the special treat of getting special attention from him.

My father always said that we were most patriotic because we love our county. We just had to work to make it better. Leonard Larsen, staff writer for *The Denver Post* quotes my father illustrating this point. "Why change the Constitution?" said Trujillo when asked how he foresaw a change in government. "The Constitution is one of the most sacred documents that America has. The Constitution calls for the protection of the welfare and the life and liberties of the people." Larsen, "Denver Communist Struggles On." *The Denver Post,* October 15, 1967.

The positive aspects of my American culture are the culturally diverse groups of people.

I Love New York City because of the diversity there. The ideals such as, democracy, peace, and freedom run closer to my value system. I love my country. It is my home and, just like in our family, we have conflicts and challenges. We have them in America and we have to strive to make things better.

My Religion

I was baptized a Catholic but I did not attend church very often. My mother prayed with me every night. She was raised a Catholic, in fact both of my parents were. I have always had a profound belief in the teaching of Christ and God, which my father at times showed disapproval of. And he would lecture me that Jesus Christ was just a good man, a revolutionary in his time.

I didn't argue with my father. I just listened to both of my parents' different points of view. I view Jesus and Marx as very similar. As a child I didn't have to read about Christ. I had him living with us. My father was a Christ figure to me. I did not go to church to get my values: I got them from my father and mother's living example. For instance, every evening there was a homeless person at our back door asking for food. We were told to fix that person a complete plate of what we had for supper. My parents always taught us to put ourselves in the other person's place.

We were taught to value and respect ourselves and people who were different, such as different races, classes cultures, sexes, and etc. For example. One time when I was five we saw a deformed man walking down the street and I was acting like the man, shaking my hand uncontrollably the way he was doing. We were in the car and my father was driving the car. He thought I was making fun of the man because my siblings laughed and he turned around and smacked me. He told me I was never to make fun of anyone! I was not making fun of him, I was just acting like him. That was the only time my father ever hit me. My father hit my older siblings and he said he was ignorant when he did that. I understood it was part of the behavior of the times that parents were able to discipline their children by hitting them. Yet I do not condone parents hitting their children.

My culture instilled in me a profound love and respect for my roots and who I am as a person.

Without my beliefs and values I would die. Life would hold very little meaning for me. That's probably why, after my father passed away, I felt like I was dying. But the moment I realized that our beliefs and values were not dead, they were very much alive in me, as they are in many people, I recovered from that thought very quickly.

I never went to a circus or a concert because we never had extra money. But one time I paid 25 cents at school and I went to a symphony at the City Auditorium. It was beautiful. I had never in my life experienced such beautiful sounds. The music stayed with me for years.

One game that my sisters and I and our closest friend, Barbara, played a lot was King and Queen. Rena was always the queen and Orlanda was always the king. I was always the maid and Barbara was the young prince. I guess even then I understood the class system and that there was the division of labor. I don't know why I was the only one who waited on them and they of course were the privileged ones. I guess because I was the youngest I played that role.

I know I am not perfect, but I am a good person. I am moral and fair. I do believe that this type of socialization, of class division can keep people down and oppressed if they do not think critically. Throughout my childhood I went back and forth questioning the existence of a God. Mother prayed with me almost every night, but my father's views made sense too. My father said, "God is a belief, and that Christ was just a man. And that Christ was a Communist who spoke out against injustices and the wrongs in society and that is why they crucified him."

My Teens

When I was about to turn fifteen my sister, Rena, and I met some nice guys in a rock and roll band. They were from Texas and they were the famous Mondo and the Chile Peppers. They were great and made a big hit here in Denver. I have a good voice and the guys in the band asked me to sing with the band. This was very exciting for me, as I loved to sing. Anyway, one night my older brother, Frank, was driving a city bus past the nightclub where I was singing and Frank knew it was my voice on the microphone that extended outside of the nightclub. So he went home and told my father. The following Sunday I walked into the club with my boyfriend, the sax player. The owner grabbed me and told me I couldn't sing there anymore because he said, "Your old man {my father} came to me and told me, if I let you in my club one more time, he will have my club shut down. And knowing your old, man he will!" That was the end of my singing career and I was really upset. But really, I had no business in there. I was only fourteen-years-old. But it sure was fun while it lasted. I still love rock and roll music.

My sister, Rena, wrote about these times. She said, "After Mondo, the leader of the band and I were introduced, Mary Lou and I would sometimes go to Corky's Corner to hear him play. Dad would take us to a movie and watch us go inside. Then we would sneak out the back and go to Corky's Corner." Like all teenagers we at times rebelled but, as you can see, it never lasted with a father like ours.

1957

I met Virgil when I was fifteen-years-old. We met at a dance in South Denver at the Soderstrom Ballroom. Virgil was twenty-one at the time, but I was a lot more mature then the average teenager. Anyway, soon after we started dating, we fell crazy in love. I liked that the guy would call me on Saturday mornings and he would be watching cartoons. He had a fine mind and he was very sensitive. He was also very good looking. Virgil and the four guys he hung around with all wore white bucks (shoes). They must have wanted to look like Pat Boom who was so popular in those days.

We went steady for a year and then he bought me an engagement ring. Virgil and his parents came to my parent' home and asked them for their permission for Virgil to marry me. This was the custom in our culture for getting parents approval. We were engaged for a year and during that year Virgil was stationed in New Orleans, Louisiana and Killeen, Texas. In 1959, two days after I graduated from high school, we were married. I was the happiest bride in the world. Two days later I left with my husband to Killeen, Texas to be with him the remaining two years he had to complete his time in the U.S. Army.

A year and three months later we were blessed with our beautiful auburn baby daughter. In 1962 we were again blessed with our darling deep dimpled son. Four years later our family was blessed with another bundle of joy, our curly black haired baby daughter.

Excerpts from my diary during that period (1969)

Where did it start, the rewarding exciting adventure into the deep tunnel of my own mind? Was I two? Was I seven? Was I twenty? It would be difficult to pinpoint. I think the volcano in me began about seven years ago, or maybe I was born with it!

I'm laying awake at night and thoughts like a force of nature keep pushing into my mind, questioning why, for what, what's it all about? I write poems. The poems reflect suffering, pain, questions, deep love, and passion.

I feel so different, because I'm Chicana, (Mexican American) born into a family who has strong beliefs in the ideology of communism.

I experience flashbacks into my childhood. I'm six again; I go to bed at night and dream of horrors, of being put in a concentration camp. I'd wake up screaming. I'm scared to death. My mother overprotects me, as she has fears of her own and I feel all her fears and I can't separate hers from mine.

What is happening to my mind? A storm is going on. It's been going on for years asking, "Who's right? Why did my father become a member of an organization that is in complete contrast to our American society?"

I went through school with a tremendous amount of drive. I had many friends. I worked very hard on my personality, an outer reflection, at times covering up of anxiety. I know why I worked so hard at being accepted. Yet I was lonely. Alienation was my friend because they don't know me.

My Crisis

After I could not have any more children and I was only twenty-seven, I went through a difficult year. Everything exploded in me. The volcano erupted. I was forced to face all of my childhood challenges and the residue of them in my adult life. My mother's abortion came back when I had to have a hysterectomy and a woman next to me who was five months pregnant was having an abortion right before my eyes. I could not understand why she would take a life and here I wanted to have more children and I couldn't have anymore. I only wanted to have six children. My mother had nine. I was devastated!

I was depressed for a year and I had a difficult time trying to figure out who I was. After that experience, I know I could live through anything. It helped to make me strong and it helped me grow. My husband's love and understanding helped me. I am thankful for my parents' love and guidance and for giving me an open mind to face reality with my own values and principles as my guide.

I am blessed with three wonderful healthy children and they replaced my grief about not having anymore. I loved my babies; they were everything to me.

I enrolled in college a year after that difficult year.

Connecting With Nature

I took a geology class. It fascinated and led me to deep thought and inner growth. On a field trip I was looking at a huge mass of ingenious rock that had been standing for billions of years. All the weaker sediments had been weathered away by erosion. I saw deep cracks in the solid mass of rock. I thought to myself. "I am that rock: the weaker parts of me have eroded away. I still have the scars (cracks) like the rocks." I observed as water drained through the cracks in the rock, just like my weaknesses drain through me. But the solid mass of strength I have gained no one will ever tear down because like the rock, I have my own power!

I am a part of the earth. The earth is solid. I am solid. I am a layer of soil compressed together and formed into a tight mass of strength and power.

I succeeded! I learned to balance the terror of being a woman, with the wonder of being a woman. I connected with nature and in doing so my belief in a universal power and my faith were enhanced.

In 1980, just before he was to have open-heart surgery, my dad betrayed his fear that he might die during surgery by talking too much and by writing a letter to his comrades. Here is excerpts of his letter:

My father's commitment to change through non-violence is clearly evident even here in what he thought might be his deathbed statement.

To all my Comrades in Colorado and in the USA,

Well, two more days, and on Wednesday morning I will have surgery to replace a blocked valve on top of my heart. I feel fine and have the greatest confidence in the people, men and women who have been tending to my care since I came in September 29th. Compared to 20 years back health care has improved very much, there is many areas still open for improvement:
We are in many areas the most advanced society in the world." Dad continues, "We indeed are the richest country in the world, but we still have not been able to get rid of these terrible problems in our society. For example, I have doctors working on me who are going to replace my heart valve with the valve of a pig. And they are doing marvelous things in the field of science and medicine, but they have not learned to remove or cure the ills of racism, war, poverty, discrimination and sexism, which is violence in its worse form.
As I lay here in this hospital bed I see the doctors are all white, and the laborers the people who bring me my food, who mop the floors, who clean and care for the patients are all mostly minorities. That is not a just system! Here at Denver General Hospital only the poor come and so you have mainly Mexicans, Indians, and Blacks and poor whites. There is not enough staff. And patients do no get adequate care. Something is basically wrong with a country that is the richest in the world and cannot care for it's entire people."

In 1990, Leonard Larsen, staff writer, for *Scripps News Service* wrote in the *Rocky Mountain News:*

The Red Empire is dissolving. The Soviet Union is shuddering from economic failure and bowing to reform. Communism itself is exposed as a useless tool in government, unable to deliver and unwilling now to even promise. I wonder what Robert Trujillo would have thought. For many years he was Colorado's one and only self-proclaimed member of the Communist Party, and he was one of the bravest, most decent and dedicated men I have ever known. I suspect that Trujillo, who died several years ago, could have accommodated communism's changed face. He wasn't one to glorify Mother Russia or any extravagant party claims of a New World. No theoretician burdened with intellectual word games, Trujillo was an honest workingman driven to communism in the brutish days of the Depression, when the coal mine shut down in southern Colorado and he was left jobless with a wife and children.

Trujillo wasn't a speaker at street corner rallies, but he did the courageous stoop labor of communism, handing out pamphlets, carrying signs and cheering bleak speeches. And all the time the FBI, police, hecklers and the news media dogged him.

Organized labor, caught up in the patriotism of the times, blacklisted Trujillo. So, in a grim bit of irony, he became a self-employed cement finisher, supporting his family and [Communist] Party work through a capitalist endeavor.

In his old age, Trujillo remained devoted to his family, his country and his cause. What also remained, reminding me of my grandfather, was a still-burning resentment of his victimization at the hands of an economic system and unfeeling government.[25]

---

[25]   Larsen, "Righteous Anger Burns Strong and Long," *Scripps News Service* printed in the *Rocky Mountain News.* Friday, October 26, 1990.

My father taught my siblings and me that the workers represent the core of American society. He said that those who serve the people on every level of our society constitute the working class, the class most discriminated against in this country. They are usually minorities and poor whites. Coal miners, farm workers, factory workers and unskilled laborers are the last to benefit from our society. Pat Bell-Blau, a communist, gives an example of the systemic racism confronting the working class in American society.

Pat wrote,

> In Pueblo [Colorado], a steel mill town 150 miles south of Denver, we formed a Party Club that held meetings against job discrimination at the Colorado Fuel and Iron Company. That company's practice of stratifying jobs according to ethnicity meant that White workers had the best-paid work, Mexi- can-Americans formed the labor gangs, and African-Americans were assigned to the coke ovens and the company-owned railway. [26]

My father devoted his life's work to these people.

During the Great Depression, Dad lost his job in the coal mine. This forced him to find alternatives in this grave economic situation. While trying to support his growing family he found himself up against a wall. He was angry and afraid. Getting involved with the masses of unemployed, he was exposed to Communist Party literature where he found some understanding of the economic condition and a direction in which to turn.

In 1982 Alan Katz, staff writer wrote in the *Denver Magazine:*

> In 1932 some fellow coal miners slipped the angry young Trujillo a copy of *The Daily Worker,* the Communist Party paper. He says that the paper opened his eyes. At that time, he was blaming local politicians

[26] Jack S. Blawis, *The Autobiography of Pat Bell-Blau* (in Progress).

and corruption for the misfortunes of people like him. 'I didn't know there was a Wall Street that was responsible for all of it,' Robert says. So, in 1935, he [Robert Trujillo] joined the [Communist] Party. He participated in the hunger marches in Washington during the 1930s, and he's been jailed six times during demonstrations in Colorado.

He's been fired from jobs because of his politics, he's had red paint splattered on his porch, he's received unfriendly visits from the FBI, but none of it seems to bother him. It only sharpens his moral outrage.[27]

Dad was adamant in his stance on being a communist. His belief in justice led him to never waiver from his commitment to building a just society, even though he endured many indignities.

As Eric Lawlor wrote in the *Rocky Mountain News*, in January, 1979:

Trujillo endured these indignities because he was a Communist at a time when being a Communist didn't win you brownie points. A lesser man would have wavered, but Trujillo kept the faith. Today, 75 and Chairman of the Colorado Communist Party, Trujillo is a respected member of the community who frequently goes before school groups to explain his views.[28]

The late 1940's and 1950's was the height of Me Carthyism. This was a time when anyone who held or advocated a point of view different from that of the American Capitalist system was considered to be a threat to this country's national

---

[27]   Alan Katz, "True Believer," *Denver Magazine*. January 1982: Vol.12, No. 2 p. 84.

[28]   Eric Lawlor, "State Communist still battling bourgeoisie," *Rocky Mountain News*, January 21, 1979.

security. There was a span of a few years during this period that Dad was expelled from the Party. The general cause was because he disagreed with the Party's liberal position on marriage. He felt there was little respect for marriage, with the only emphasis on the Party. As the anti-Communist hysteria faded after World War II, he was reinstated into the Party. And in the 1960's he felt honored to serve as the Chairman of the Colorado Communist Party.

During the Civil Rights Movement the tensions around the nation were creating mass demonstrations against the war in Vietnam, protests for jobs, equal education, housing and poverty. The Civil Rights Movement was an assertion of the equal rights of Blacks, Latinos, Native Americans and poor people of all colors. Dad was in the heat of it all and he continued to practice and teach about socialism and communism because he continued to see injustice and discrimination. The war in Vietnam was a prime example. No event in recent history has left such lasting negative effects on United States foreign policy, as did the intervention in Vietnam. The people of the United States and around the world questioned the reasons for the war. As the government demanded greater support for extending the war, the people intensified their opposition. My father was one of those who opposed the war.

The one constant in Dad's life was his commitment to the struggle against racism and injustice, and he found a lot of satisfaction in sticking his neck out for those who seldom have a voice.

The time, energy and conviction that Dad directed towards the struggle made him happy, as was illustrated during an interview with Dad. In 1975, in The Rocky Mountain News Charles Roos, wrote: "Was Robert happy? He called himself the Happy Communist. He is, by his own description, a 'happy' Communist. Robert, calling for 'real democracy and freedom' in the United States, referred to this country as 'our beloved nation.'[29]

---

[29]   Charles Roos, "At 71, Denverite Is Happy He's A Communist," *The Rocky Mountain News,* Sunday, August 3, 1975

My father was happy many times, and many times he was not. He carried tremendous responsibility throughout his life. He did it well and he did it his way. He was a revolutionary with a vision to create a world of true humanity. His gift of clarity and analysis took him to places that many do not care to go. He never accepted injustices and he never failed to speak out and act against them. It was his quest for the truth that motivated him to become a revolutionary.

Readers of this book must set aside preconceived notions about communism and poor people. Written material about communism is usually biased, either anti-communist or pro-communist. Generally, communist theory values life, humanity, knowledge, justice, courage, temperance, compassion, and, mainly, love. In my opinion, it would be a better world if more people would value truth, justice, peace, and love.

The following are excerpts from Pat Bell-Blau's autobiography about her experience during the McCarthy period:

> I was still asleep when Vicente, [a comrade] knocked at the door. "I got a call from Denver last night," he said, as he sat down on the edge of a chair. Embarrassment showed in his weather-beaten face. 'A1 said to tell you to get out of town."
>
> 'What for?' 'I don't know, Pat, that's all A1 Said.' Vicente looked at me earnestly. "There's something funny going on up there."
>
> "It must be something important," I said. "Anyway A1 wouldn't call like that on his own. It must have been a decision." Vicente agreed. Good friends and comrades, we were joined by mutual respect, and he knew I'd be sore at being ordered out of Trinidad [Colorado] so suddenly.
>
> "Vicente, please tell Joe [Gurule] what happened." "I will, but it's not going to be easy."
>
> He said good-bye quickly, and when he was gone I got dressed, stuffed a brush and comb and toothbrush into my purse, and went out into the bright September sun in southern Colorado. I had $12 and

no transportation. The bus station seemed the best bet, but there they told me no bus would leave until the afternoon. El Capitan (the captain) would take me to Albuquerque, where there were friends, so I bought a ticket with $ 8 of my assets.

The train ride to Albuquerque gave me a chance to think. I should have seen Joe before I left Trinidad. He was the Progressive Party candidate for Congress in the southern Colorado district, and I had been his campaign manager up to that point. Right then Joe looked like a winner. He was secretary-treasurer of his United Mine Workers local in the area that coals the steel mill now known as Colorado Fuel and Iron. The Ludlow Massacre of 1914, in which the wives and children of striking miners were intentionally killed by Rockefeller thugs, had made a bad name out of Rockefeller Fuel and Iron.

It was a region that had seen many organizing battles. In 1927, when a strike of all coal miners in Colorado was called because miners demanded a six-hour day, a five-day week, and a basic daily wage of $7.75, six men were killed and sixty injured, including women and children.

Tranquilino Gurule, Joe's father, had been a UMWA [United Mine Workers of America] organizer, beloved by miners throughout the region. The family had come home more than once to find their home vandalized or burned, a Union leader tobacco can nailed to a tree to emphasize the warning. Joe knew just about every miner in that congressional district, and all of their problems in supporting their families.

I just hoped someone would help Joe to carry out the schedule of meetings we'd set up. The election was only two months off, and voting a third-party ticket was a new idea that took a lot of explaining, even if it was for Gurule.

Nationally, the Progressive party was begun by voters who could see little difference between the presidential programs of the two parties. Unlike Truman and Dewey, Wallace decried talk of war with the USSR. He argued for the acceptance of world disarmament proposals. Protest against President Truman's war-like actions was nationwide, and Wallace's campaign for the White House was picking up steam. The Progressives had elected a congressman, Stanley Aaronson, at a special election in New York, and Wallace had drawn a crowd of 48,000 at a meeting in Yankee Stadium, the largest political gathering ever seen in New York City. The Saturday Evening Post ran the headline, "How the Reds Snatched Henry Wallace." But Wallace was not a communist, although the Communist Party was giving him its support, and was the best organized among the varied groups of farmers, workers, veterans, and intellectuals who bought the program.

When I left the train in Albuquerque and walked past the Pueblo Indian women displaying their jewelry on the platform, I was too preoccupied to stop and admire their work as usual. I couldn't imagine why I should have been taken out of the campaign just as it was gaining momentum.

But as I walked down Central Avenue, there on a rack was a newspaper that told me all I needed to know. Under the headline, "Missing Mystery Woman," was an old picture of me, and the accompanying story said that my husband and two Denver comrades, Jane Rogers and Nancy Wertheim had been jailed for refusal to cooperate with a Federal Court grand jury probing "Communist activity in Denver." The authorities had noticed, as we had, that our campaign had a chance of success, and they were out to sabotage it with the Red smear tactic.

I took the paper into a coffee shop and read that my husband, Irving Blau, 34, had been sentenced to six months for refusing to answer questions on my whereabouts.

The stated purpose of the hearing was to "investigate Communism" at a nearby Air Force base, activity which the government knew as well as I did was nonexistent. [After three months of living underground, I returned to Denver to get my two daughters thinking it would be safe by then. Early in December I went to the main post office, having received notice to pick up a registered mail. The main post office of that era was also the Federal courthouse. I was asked to wait for my package, and after an unusually long wait for my package, a U.S. marshal appeared and handed me a subpoena. It required my appearance before the grand jury, on January 4, 1949. [Pat appeared in court.]

Hour after hour, the U.S. attorney read lists of names as if from a phonebook. After each name, he asked me to state whether that person was a member of the Communist Party. Once in a while a familiar name was tossed in of a comrade, of the mayor of Denver, or of a prominent Republican. The game was to trick the witness into a spontaneous answer, then declare the witness's right to refuse answers had been waived. In the late afternoon I was taken before Judge Symes. The judge ordered me to answer some of the questions, which I refused [to answer] in the grand jury room.

He warned that I could be found guilty of contempt if I continued to reject the questions. Once again, I repeated that although my political activity was all on the public record, I could not answer any questions, but had to maintain my right against self-incrimination, in view of the criminal case against the Communist Party leadership, which the government was then pursuing.

I was sent to the Denver County Jail, and met in a friendly way by the prisoners there. They also were victims of class justice, and responded instinctively when one refused to be an informer.

"Mrs. Patricia Blau, object of a three-months-long search by a grand jury investigating Communism, was sentenced yesterday by U.S. Judge J.Foster Symes to a year in jail for criminal contempt." *The Denver Post* (January 5, 1949).

Nearly two years later, in December 1950, the U.S. Supreme Court would by a vote of 8–0 reverse the conviction and void the sentence. They agreed that I was within my constitutional right to refuse to testify, seeing that national leaders of the Communist Party had been indicted under the Smith Act.

Time Magazine disapproved of the court's action.

Time published a picture of me along with that of Aaron Burr, and quoted Justice Hugo Black as having recalled "Chief Justice John Marshall's famed ruling reaffirming this guarantee of the Fifth Amendment in the Burr treason trial." From Mr. Burr to Mrs. Blau the constitutional line was clear... The court's latest decision also brought into sharp question the constitutionality of the McCarran anti-subversive act, which Communists are currently defying. Forcing a person to register as a Communist might also conceivably be held an infringement of his rights under the Fifth Amendment." *Time* magazine, 25 December 1950. For the Supreme Court decision verbatim, see *Current History,* February, 1951.

In a chapter "A Window on the Time—Cold War at Home" Pat Blau wrote a reflection of her thoughts about McCarthy:

No one can hope to understand this story who does not know something of how the Cold War, launched against a foreign power soon after World War II, was next turned against citizens of the United States. Loss and suffering were inflicted on them without due process of law, and the protection the victims got from their civil rights was at first amazingly small.

Much dust has been thrown in the eyes of those who have sought to understand that period. The first thing the persistent seeker must do is to expel from vocabulary and consciousness the names and the ideas "McCarthy" and "McCarthyism." McCarthy was real enough in his day, but since his death in 1957, he and the "ism" have been converted into mythology, greatly exaggerated in importance, to make it seem that one man and his philosophy embodied the whole assault on the Bill of Rights.

McCarthy was simply an opportunist who latched onto the anti-Communism of his betters, hoping thus to be propelled to the heights they had reached. McCarthy must be forgotten, and attention concentrated on Truman and Eisenhower and their appointees. John Foster Dulles and Herbert Brownell did more harm in five minutes than McCarthy did in his lifetime."

Pat added, this period of repression, the Smith Act, and the McCarran Act during the McCarthy era did catastrophic damage to the Party, including its self-destruction in some areas, such as Grant County, New Mexico."

On January 21, 1979, staff writer, Eric Lawlor, wrote about Robert in *The Rocky Mountain News:* "Times have certainly changed. Twenty years ago [Robert Trujillo was] routinely threatened and spat at; kept awake at nights by obscene telephone calls; his home daubed with red paint and his children victimized at school. 'People thought that because you were a communist you were a foreign agent,' said Trujillo, 'but you learn to live with the suspicion and the treats and the slurs.' Lawlor, "State Communist Still Battling Bourgeoisie," *The Rocky Mountain News*, January 21, 1997.

An example of one of the many insults that Dad tolerated took place while he was a guest speaker in a class at Bear Creek High School in the eighties. A student in the class where Dad was speaking spit in his coffee. Responding to the letter of apology (the student was probably instructed by the teacher to write it.) Robert wrote:

Dear Terry, Student at Bear Creek High School, I have received your undated letter in which you apologize for having spit in my cup of coffee at Bear Creek High School on October 20, 1982. You state in your letter that you got mad because I would not agree with our system of government in the U.S.A. The U.S. Constitution gives all of its citizens the right to oppose, criticize and/or condemn any wrongdoings committed against them by their established governmental bodies. Your despicable act of spitting in my coffee is a very mild act in comparison to what our government is doing against the welfare and economic security of two hundred and twenty some million people in this nation and to many other millions all over the world. For example: Capitalism is based on production for profits and huge corporations hold the means of production as private ownership. The end result of such planning is that millions of people are thrown out of work, millions lose their homes, and millions starve to death both physically and mentally.

Can this be a "Good System of Government" when, for example, we have a U.S. senator in Washington, Ted Kennedy, who has accumulated so much wealth that he can agree to give his wife four million dollars in a divorce settlement case? When billions of dollars are squandered away on armaments to be used to perpetuate in power a system that exploits and oppresses millions and millions of human being? Witness what happened in Cuba and Nicaragua and is now happening in El Salvador, other Latin American nations, Africa, and in the Middle East. Capitalism is a monster with a brain the size of a peanut!

The major news media, owned operated and controlled by the wealthy corporations, keep people ignorant of the fact that Communists in the U.S.A. were the sponsors and leaders in organizing the struggles during the Depression. For example, Communists and other leftist organizations were instrumental in forcing the government to create jobs through programs such as the (W.P.A., etc.), 'Works Project Administration'. We were also able to get the government to establish Weekly Unemployment Insurance, State and Federal Pensions (Social Security), and welfare benefits.

The solutions to the problems caused by the system of "Man-Must-Exploit Man" are Unity and Struggle! The people do not want any more wars! They appreciate the cheese but they want jobs, not bombs. * (Referring to the free cheese the government was giving out to those in need during that period.)

Because we, in the Communist Party, immensely appreciate the respect that is held for The constitutional right of "Freedom of Speech" by your teachers and the Jefferson County School Board, we therefore send them a copy of this letter.

I, personally, without hate or prejudice, do accept your apology.

Sincerely,

Robert Trujillo, Chairman of the Colorado Communist Party.

Here is an examples of my father's stance on injustices and non-violence that stand out in my mind.

First, I remember that during the McCarthy era when all communists were being rounded up and prosecuted, journalist, Charles Roos said of Dad during that era that, "He [Robert Trujillo] somehow escaped in the 1950's when the federal government was prosecuting communist officials in wholesale lots for plotting to overthrow the government by force and violence. Indeed it would be difficult at least in 1975, to associate Roberto Trujillo with violence. A bomb would look as out of place in his hand as a polo mallet." Roos, "At 71, Denverite Is Happy He's A Communist," *The Rocky, Mountain News,* Sunday, August 3, 1975.

Barbara Revelle at the celebration

"Mr. Trujillo led a difficult life, a life of struggle and pain. He grew up in the Depression. Lost two brothers to malnutrition and lost a son and grandson. He was a sheepherder and a coal miner, but all that never defeated him. He wasn't a quitter. He was a survivor.

And probably those times gave him the power—the spirit—and the anger to stand up for what he believed in. We can call what he believed in by many different names and some of those names make people nervous—and one of those names is Communist

"There were also controversies surrounding the Ludlow Massacre and the Massacre at Sand Creek. There are people in the mural from both sides. Again they questioned, 'Why do we have to represent these things. We're not proud of these incidents of racism and hatred.' Revelle says the mural is not a whitewash. "It's very important to represent those struggles and to show that everything wasn't always terrific and nice here. A lot of people had to pay the price with their lives and sometimes for the work they did."

The anti-Communist movement grew during the labor struggle of the 1930's due to the identification of Communists in the Congress of Industrial Organizations, (CIO) which emphasized cross- industrial organizations. This tactic of Red baiting, accusing the new unions of being run by Reds, made it easy to confront unions thus taking attention away from the larger economic issues. As the American "Others" (progressives) were becoming politicized and identifying with communism, including the party's Moscow connection, this conveniently fit the anti-Communist movement's agenda with the 'fear of foreigners.' Since the founding on the nation, those who were identified as foreign-born radicals had been a target of persecution. Men and women who had made outstanding contributions and progressive advances, like those who helped to organize and form unions for the labor movement, were exiled.

American anti-Communism, known as the nations' counter-subversive tradition, was the irrational belief that anyone that held different political views, such as political dissidents, foreigners, or members of racial and religious minorities, threatened the nation. See Ellen Schrecker, The Age of McCarthvism: A Brief History With Documents. (Boston: St. Martin's Press, 1994)

My mother used to say, "Cada cabeza es un mundo." Meaning that every mind (head) is a world of its own. My siblings each have their own story of growing up "Red." Each of us lived in a world of our own. Born into the same family at different times, we each had our own unique experience when it came to living out our life in a Mexican/American, Communist family. But the one constant in all of our lives was that our father, throughout his life, remained devoted to the causes of world peace and justice, blessing all of us with these values. How each of us experienced our father and his values is as varied and unique as is each of our individual minds.

1979

In 1979 Robert wrote to Senator Edward Kennedy concerning Kennedy's Senate Bill #1722 which had been introduced in Congress. This bill had an even greater burden on the poor and the working class by increasing penalties, adding new Federal crimes and many other restrictions.

The following is the letter to Senator Edward Kennedy.

November 2, 1979

United States Senator Edward Kennedy

Dear Senator Edward Kennedy:

I am aware and concerned about Senate Bill # 1722 that you have sponsored and introduced in Congress.

This Bill if enacted into law will do away with the most sacred rights that we now have under the Constitution of the United States. It is a fascist piece of legislation that the American people will not accept passively.

The citizens of this nation are not even given the benefit or their access to nation-wide hearings to present their views on this tricky piece of legislation.

The media lets us know that you are about to announce your candidacy for President of the United States.

Does history teach you anything Senator Kennedy? What will be the reaction of individuals acting alone on the feelings and reactions of the general population who will suffer the consequences and repression that will surely come down on us all?

History surely must teach you and us especially, what has happened in our nation and in the world when Democracy is not allowed to flourish? Witness [if you will] the ugly atmosphere created by the 1929 Depression just 50 years ago, the McCarthy period, the cold blooded and unjust murders of your two brothers, President John F. Kennedy and Senator Robert Kennedy. Furthermore lets look at Iran, Nicaragua, Batista in Cuba, Chile, South Korea and not the least Czarist Russia, the Hitler—Nazi Holocaust and etc.?

When will we learn and take to heart, the advice of Pope Paul II and Fidel Castro, to work for World Peace, a world free of Greed, Hunger, Inflation, Unemployment, Racism, Ku Klux Klan poison that divides and destroys humanity!

Yours very truly,

Robert Trujillo

> My big surprise was finding out about the system in the Soviet Union where there were many differences that interested me. In time, and to learn more about these differences in political systems, my wife and I made two trips to the Soviet Union. And in 1980, my wife and I visited Cuba to learn more about conditions in that newly formed socialist nation. In both visits I saw for myself there were no slums because there was no unemployment. Every citizen who was willing and able to work had a job. People who were sick and disabled were given proper care and treatment at no cost plus sufficient income to sustain them. All of it was based on humanitarian conception and everyone was expected to work, if able, or forfeit the right to eat.
>
> Under the capitalists system the very wealthy do not have to work. In fact the super rich do not even pay income taxes yet they enjoy the best food in the world. Poor people in the capitalist countries are confronted with high rents, high food costs, exorbitant prices for necessities, and cheap foods that fill the body with bulk and empty calories. This, I found, is the real truth in the basic differences between the

two systems, capitalism and socialism, a truth you cannot find in reports we get from our commercial media.

The following article came out in the *Denver Post* on Wednesday, May 7, 1969:

The chamber was cleared of the 14 demonstrators. Policeman carried thirteen of the demonstrators out, two policemen to a demonstrator. The demonstration was peaceful. Seventeen unarmed officers entered the chamber at 11:31 a.m. and the chamber was kept locked until the officers arrived. Only senators and reporters were allowed to enter. As the police entered, one of the demonstrators said to the group: 'OK. Link up.' They all joined arms and began making separate statements first declaring after the linkup: 'We are interposing our bodies on the American conscience.' One of the younger male demonstrators, when it came his turn to make a statement directed his remarks to police who stood below the speaker platform and allowed them to make their orations. He said. "You can take off your helmets because were not going to come to you. We love you." Two or three of the group called Hogan by his first name. One of them said, "We know how you feel: It's those other people out there." A spokesman also thanked Senator George Brown, D-Denver and several other Democratic members of the Senate for remaining in the chamber. 'At least you stayed around and listened to us,' he said to Brown. 'Were going to stay here until you pass meaningful legislation. We don't care how long it takes.' Most of the demonstrators apparently participated in a quiet protest on the first floor of the Capitol Tuesday when they carried in several empty boxes [Symbolizing] resembling coffins to observe defeat of legislation they reported. ("14 Arrested For Halting State Senate," *The Denver Post* 7 May 1969.

In 1970, Rykken Johnson, wrote "13 Demonstrators Freed in State Protest."

> "The verdict of the three-man three-woman jury was returned at 2:45 p.m. Friday. Nearly six hours of study were required before the jury reached a decision. The fourteen demonstrators were accused of unlawful assembly and willful obstruction of a messenger or official of the state of Colorado after they entered Senate chambers to protest what they termed the Legislature's lack of action on social welfare issues. Testimony during the trial, which started Jan. 16, came from senators, police who were summoned to remove the demonstrators and from Lieutenant Gov. Mark Hogan, who was conducting the session. Hogan said he called for a recess of the Senate while the protesters were entering the chambers. They did not leave upon request and he called police, Hogan testified. There was noticeable relief when Judge Alexander read the first decision to the Reverend Joseph Craig Hart. 'We the jury find the defendant not guilty...of the complaint filed herein,' he read as each of the thirteen defendants stood to hear the verdict.

Defendants, Friends Jubilant

There was pandemonium in the courtroom. The defendants were hugging, and then kissing everyone who came close. There was shouting, laughter, back pounding, and then singing. 'We Shall Overcome' filtered down the almost- deserted hallway outside the packed courtroom, where a Denver County Court jury had just acquitted thirteen of the Denver fourteen. Someone looked for Judge Gilbert Alexander, but he had retired, leaving the courtroom to the wildly cheering defendants and the spectators.

Even before the verdict was read, the defendants had a written statement for the press. But the statement, written by the Reverend Austin Warner, 49, was composed so that it could be used, whatever the verdicts. Before giving The Denver Post the typewritten pages the Reverend Warner, one of the fourteen charged in the takeover last May of the Colorado Senate, tore the first paragraph off. That paragraph had been written in case the jury returned a guilty verdict.

"Our confidence in the judicial process has been confirmed," the statement said, "and our hopes for the democratic system strengthened. What concerns us most, however, is the overriding cause of our effort. We still must keep uppermost in our minds the people whose voice is still unheard in the halls and chambers of the State Capital.

Hispanic Farm laborers continue to live in poverty," the statement said, "while children of migrants are more malnourished than those in many underdeveloped countries of the world. Collective bargaining is denied those who work in fields and greenhouses, and thousands of minorities' poor' live in the city ghettos."

'The 47th Colorado General Assembly "Killed more than 20 bills that would help rectify these conditions," the statement charged. "We therefore call upon the governor again, the legislators and, indeed, all the people of our state who care for the common good of all to place in our highest priority these needs of the poor and minorities that have been so grossly ignored," the statement said.

The judge had read the verdicts separately. After the last defendant was pronounced innocent, the judge asked Terry Wiggins, deputy district attorney prosecuting the case, if he wanted a poll of the jury. "Yes, your honor, I do," Wiggins said, and the jurors individually repeated their decisions orally. After a few moments of final jury instructions, Judge Alexander adjourned the court, and the uproar was unleashed." Johnson, ["13 Demonstrators Freed In State Protest," *The Rocky Mountain News*, 25 January 1970.]

CPSIA information can be obtained
at www.ICGtesting.com
Printed in the USA
FSHW022123080619
58847FS